# THE DANGEROUS DIVIDE

## ALSO BY PETER EICHSTAEDT

*Above the Din of War: Afghans Speak About Their Lives, Their Country, and Their Future—and Why America Should Listen*

*Consuming the Congo: War and Conflict Minerals in the World's Deadliest Place*

*First Kill Your Family: Child Soldiers of Uganda and the Lord's Resistance Army*

*If You Poison Us: Uranium and Native Americans*

*Pirate State: Somalia's Terrorism at Sea*

# THE DANGEROUS DIVIDE

★ ★ ★

## PERIL AND PROMISE ON THE US-MEXICO BORDER

PETER EICHSTAEDT

Lawrence Hill Books
Chicago

Published by Lawrence Hill Books
An imprint of Chicago Review Press Incorporated
814 North Franklin Street
Chicago, Illinois 60610
ISBN 978-1-61374-836-7


**Library of Congress Cataloging-in-Publication Data**
Eichstaedt, Peter H., 1947–
 The dangerous divide : peril and promise on the US-Mexico border / Peter
Eichstaedt.
   pages cm
 Includes index.
 ISBN 978-1-61374-836-7
 1. Mexican-American Border Region. 2. Border security—Mexican-American
Border Region. 3. Illegal aliens—United States. 4. Crime—Mexican-American
Border Region. 5. United States—Emigration and immigration—Government
policy. 6. Mexico—Emigration and immigration—Government policy. I. Title.
 JV6565.E43 2014
 364.1'370973—dc23
                              2014002430


Interior design: Jonathan Hahn
Map design: Chris Erichsen
Photos: © Peter Eichstaedt

Printed in the United States of America
5 4 3 2 1

The mission bells told me, that I shouldn't stay.
South of the border, down Mexico way.

—From "South of the Border (Down Mexico Way)"
*Written by Kennedy/Carr*

# CONTENTS

## PART IV: THE ENFORCERS

## PART V: BREWING A SOLUTION

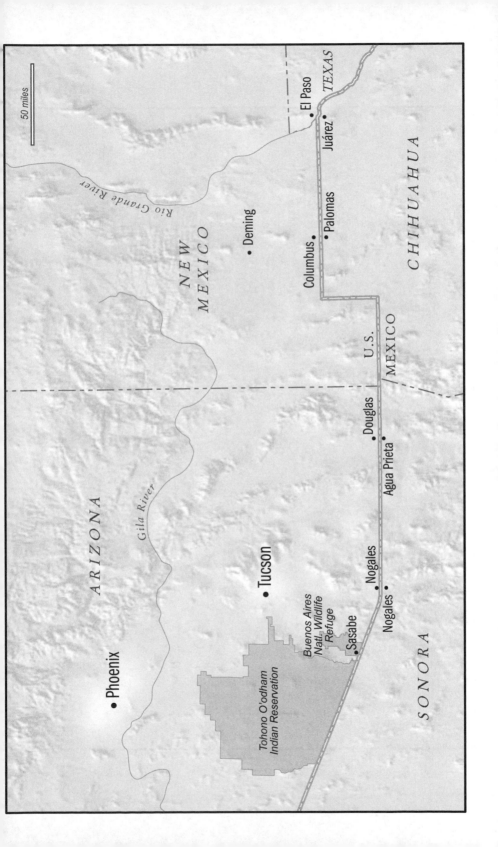

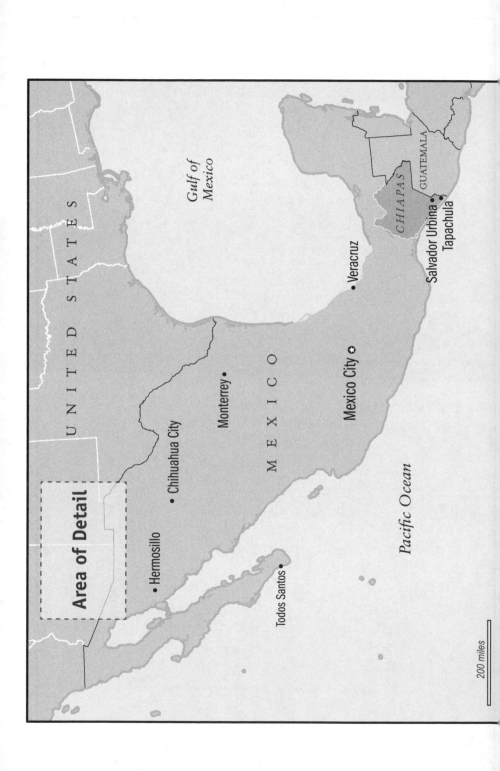

Area of Detail

UNITED STATES

Gulf of
Mexico

• Hermosillo

• Chihuahua City

• Monterrey

M E X I C O

• Todos Santos

• Veracruz

Mexico City ✪

Pacific Ocean

CHIAPAS

GUATEMALA

Salvador Urbina •
Tapachula

200 miles

# PROLOGUE

✵

**A**fter a flurry of packing, my suitcase was heaved into the belly of a
Greyhound bus filled with students eager to say good-bye to the
dreary dampness of the Columbus, Ohio, winter. It was early January
1967, just after the Christmas holiday break, and I was a sophomore at
Ohio State University on my way to Mexico.

Months earlier my roommate had asked if I was interested in join-
ing him in a program where OSU students spent a few months living
and studying at the University of the Americas in Mexico City with
full credit for classes. Great, I thought. It was something that I could
easily fit into my studies, which at the time were aimless.

The war in Vietnam was heating up, and draft-eligible young men
like me who were not in school were on their way to army boot camp.
Antiwar protests were a regular occurrence and increasingly violent.
The following year, 1968, America would convulse, perhaps changing
forever. The Olympic Games in Mexico City would see black-gloved
fists raised in protest against racism even as Alabama governor George
Wallace campaigned to be president. Two American heroes, Robert F.
Kennedy and Martin Luther King Jr., would die from assassins' bullets.
The Democratic and Republican Party conventions in Chicago and
Miami, respectively, would devolve into clouds of tear gas and flailing
nightsticks. It was a good time to get out of the country for a while. As

the war in Vietnam dragged on, chances were good that I'd be going sooner or later. When I asked my parents if I could go to Mexico, they readily agreed.

My prior contact with Mexico and Mexicans had been nonexistent. I had grown up in the farm belt of southern Michigan surrounded by fields of towering sweet corn, wide rows of luscious strawberries, and leafy orchards of trees laden with apples, peaches, and pears. The crops and fruit were picked by families of seasonal workers from Mexico, who for the most part kept to themselves. My notions of Mexico had been shaped by cartoon characters like Speedy Gonzales, comedian Jose Jimenez, and postcard caricatures of sandal-clad men with large sombreros sleeping against saguaro cacti.

At Laredo, Texas, we crossed into Mexico and I felt the thrill of finally entering foreign territory. After a lunch in a cavernous restaurant in Monterrey filled with plants, birds, and music, we rolled through the dark mountains, passing other buses on winding roads and around blind curves. The next morning, we arrived in Mexico City. Alive and well.

I roamed the city freely during those months and learned the pleasures of *mole* sauce and soft tacos filled with minced pork—a far cry from the fare found in Mexican restaurants across the American Southwest. I wandered the expanses of the Zócalo plaza in the heart of the city; drifted in the floating gardens of Xochimilco; climbed the stone Aztec pyramids of Teotihuacán; and marveled at the mariachi mecca of Plaza Garibaldi. I frequented the stunning Museum of Natural History, home to grand stone artifacts of the Toltecs and Aztecs, including the mystical Mayan calendar.

I returned home with a head full of Central and South American history and culture and a basic knowledge of Spanish. Mexico felt comfortable, if not familiar, and I would return.

In the mid-1970s, I settled in Santa Fe, New Mexico, drawn by its Southwestern lifestyle saturated with the culture and history of Mexico. Founded in about 1610 by Spanish explorers who rode north from Mexico City, Santa Fe is a blend of the Native American cultures of the ageless pueblos along the Rio Grande, the centuries of Spanish and Mexican rule, and the coming of the Anglo-Americans.

I worked for the *New Mexican* newspaper, established in 1849, making it the oldest daily newspaper west of the Mississippi River. I rummaged the musty archives from when the newspaper was printed in Spanish and English with stories of outlaws, shootouts, and cattle rustlers. An entire issue was dedicated to the infamous 1916 raid by Mexican revolutionary Pancho Villa on Columbus, New Mexico, a dusty town on the Mexico border.

My wife and I bought land southeast of town in Apache Canyon and built an adobe brick house using passive solar heating design. The canyon was the site of the westernmost battle of the Civil War, in which a union force destroyed a Confederate convoy seeking a secure route to California goldfields.

As I prowled Santa Fe for cheap adobe bricks, I found myself on a large gravel lot piled high with them. Garage-sized rooms made of concrete blocks flanked the brickyard and housed families of Mexican migrants who made what I was about to buy. For the first time I realized the deep economic and social impact Mexican migrant labor has on American life. The bricks were the cheapest in town, and despite my reservations about supporting what was most likely illegal labor and profits, I bought them.

A decade on, with America's surging demand for drugs, Mexico was no longer the carefree getaway but a corridor for South American cocaine. Santa Fe changed from a bucolic artist colony to a chic destination for the rich and famous. Shops selling high-end Santa Fe–style furniture, clothing, Native American rugs, pottery, and turquoise jewelry were sandwiched between art galleries displaying desert landscapes. Once a historic outpost at the end of the Santa Fe Trail, it soon resembled a stucco outdoor shopping mall. And for a while in the town's slick nightspots, one could sniff cocaine off the bar while sipping Russian vodka and sucking down fresh raw oysters.

After two decades in Santa Fe and the end of my marriage, I packed my bags and headed for Mexico. Solace and distance, I was sure, would help me come to grips with what had happened and what lay ahead. From El Paso, a twin-engine turboprop landed on the cracked asphalt tarmac in Chihuahua, where I took a deep breath of the warm, gritty air. Signs of the war on drugs were everywhere. My bag was sniffed by a guard dog, then x-rayed and rifled by a couple of belligerent, heavily armed soldiers.

A day later, I stepped off the train in the town of Creel, where timber was stacked along the tracks. I made my way across the plaza with its well-kept gazebo to a bed and breakfast guesthouse filled with Europeans that offered a communal dinner and conversation in several languages. As one of the few Americans, I joined the nightly groping for words to make myself understood.

I teamed with other travelers to hire the battered Chevy Suburbans with mismatched tires parked on the plaza that took us to mountain waterfalls and Tarahumara villages where the natives consumed copious amounts of their homemade brew. One day we descended into a steep canyon following a winding footpath to a hot springs pool and soaked in piping-hot mineral spring water. We cooled in the shallows of a stream that traced the canyon floor and stretched out on the wide, smooth boulders to sleep in the sun. The world felt very far away.

The train ended in the Mexican coastal port town of Los Mochis, Sinaloa, a smugglers' haven. Hoping to catch the overnight passenger boat to La Paz on the Baja peninsula, I was told it was sold out. I took a taxi to the airport and bought the last seat on the next flight to La Paz, where I negotiated with a taxi driver to take me across the Baja to the tiny town of Todos Santos, or "all saints," a sleepy artist colony and retreat on the Pacific coast. He dropped me off at the portal of the Hotel California, said to be the namesake of the song made famous by the Eagles.

The hotel was strangely empty, save for the bartender, Juan. I climbed onto a stool in the narrow bar where Juan poured me a tall shot of Hornitos, pried the cap off a Corona, and turned up the volume to the Eagles album. It was late spring, Juan explained, well past spring break time when college students descend, and too early for the fishing and diving crowd. Perfect, I said, and downed the tequila, which Juan immediately replenished. Photos, hats, license plates, and other memorabilia left by those who had made the road trip from Southern California to Todos Santos covered the walls. After a week, I was sated with sun, sand, and tequila. I headed back to Santa Fe.

It would be another fifteen years before I would return to Mexico to write this book. In the interim, I lived and worked in the Balkans, Eastern Europe, the Caucasus, Africa, and Afghanistan. I wrote about the Ugandan madman Joseph Kony and his army of child soldiers. I met and talked with pirates of Somalia and spent time among the three hundred thousand Somalis who filled the world's largest refugee camp, having fled the bloodshed and strife in their ancient homeland. I walked the misty hills of Masisi in the eastern Congo, where brutal militias remained locked in a bloody quest to control highly prized minerals vital to the high-tech dependency of the Western world.

During 2010 and 2011, as I worked in Kabul, Afghanistan, for the Institute for War and Peace Reporting, I crisscrossed Afghanistan interviewing the forgotten Afghans who suffered as global powers wrestled to pacify a land called the graveyard of empires. Yet I followed the news coming out of Mexico of the daily violence that far outstripped the war in Afghanistan; the death toll was markedly higher, the deaths more gruesome. While suicide bombers obliterated themselves in the name of Allah, cartel gunmen and executioners cut off heads in front of video cameras and hung bodies from highway bridges, all in the name of drugs and fear. Some soaked their enemies in oil and burned them alive in fifty-gallon drums.

The horrifying death toll mounting in America's backyard had gone virtually unreported even as Americans each day used products made in Mexico, ate food grown in Mexico, drove cars assembled in Mexico, drank Mexican tequila and beer, and crowded into Mexican restaurants. Americans had been told little about their neighboring country's plight, yet were provided regular updates about the killings in Afghanistan and Pakistan. Mexico had become a terra incognita.

When I returned to the United States in the fall of 2011, my thoughts returned to Mexico, the land and people who had gone from being America's neighbor to a threat to life and liberty. Arizona adopted Senate Bill 1070 sanctioning law enforcement to check immigration papers of anyone suspected to be in the country illegally. The people who cut the grass, picked the crops, built and cleaned the houses, and cooked the food in most restaurants were vilified as "illegal aliens."

What had happened to the country and borderlands that many Americans, including myself, long held near and dear? To answer that question, I traveled the borderlands of the Southwest meeting with people about how life had changed, why, and what could be done to restore the balance and relations we once had.

I looked at America's borderlands not with jaundiced eyes, but with eyes that have witnessed how much all humans share regardless of their circumstances. We want a fair chance at life and to die in peace. We want love and lives with family and friends. We want our children to grow and learn and find their own way as strong and capable people. We want justice for ourselves and for others, and in the end to know that our lives meant something.

By returning to the Southwest, I came full circle. After leaving a dozen years earlier to live, work, and write about some of the most troubled corners of the planet, I found that America's legendary borderlands had become a frontier of fear. This book is neither a comprehensive policy analysis nor an exposé of the Mexican drug cartels. Plenty has been written on that already. Rather, I roamed the roiling borderlands and found they have become something that few could have imagined. I hope this exploration helps us find a way out of America's immigrant morass, which punishes only those who want nothing more than a chance at the American dream, the same dream that we all cherish and protect.

# I

★ ★ ★

# THE MIGRANTS

# I

# DESERT SOLITAIRE

※

**R**oberto stands on the gritty hillside in the southern Arizona desert, eight miles from the Mexico border. The sun is high and hot, heavy on his shoulders. He sighs, scanning the dirt, spiky cactus, and spindly mesquite for signs of life. Fear sweeps over him.

*Where are they? Where are my amigos? I hate this place. So dry. Not like my town on the banks of the Lake Atitlán in Guatemala. In the mountains, so cool and green. These are not like my mountains, the volcanoes of Atitlán, San Pedro, and Tolimán. These are dry and offer nothing but death. But I will not die. I cannot die. Mi esposa, mis niños, my wife and children. They need me. They depend on me. That is why I came to this terrible place.*

Roberto tries to swallow, but his throat is dry. He shuffles along the dirt in his worn and loose high-top shoes, then settles in the mottled shade of the mesquite. He opens his pack. The water bottles are empty. He pushes clothes aside. Half a bag of white Wonder Bread. Flour tortillas wrapped in a plastic bag.

*I can't swallow. I need water.*

Roberto closes his backpack, hoists it to his shoulder, and angles down the slope. His steps are slow, deliberate. He pauses to check for the sound of voices, of vehicles, of *la migra*, the border police.

*It has been three days now. They came overhead in the dark of night. How could they see us? How did they know? The helicopter shook the air and blew the dirt like a storm. It came down very close. We were scared, and then they were there, the border police,* la migra, *waiting. I scrambled up the hillside and disappeared into the night.*

Roberto pauses just one hundred yards from murky water, a ranch pond made for cattle. There is no one, not even the cows. The wind moves slowly, rustling leaves. He walks to where the mud has dried and cracked. He opens one of the plastic bottles, squats, and tilts it under the surface. The murky water gurgles in, a yellowish orange. He holds the bottle to his mouth, but the scent repels him. Yet he sips.

*It is warm but not so bad.*

He fills the bottle, and then another, stands, and picks up his pack.

*I have twenty-three years and I am strong and I can work hard. That is all I want. I am good with my hands and my back is strong. I am good with a shovel. In America, el Norte, there is work. I know I will find some. In my town of Panajachel there is nothing. New York, Nueva York. The great city in America. That is where I will go. It is my dream.*

Roberto retraces his steps up the hill then settles in the shade, where he searches his pack for the bag of bread. He folds a couple of slices and takes a bite, chewing slowly. Roberto wets his mouth with a swig of the yellowed water, just enough to swallow. His stomach knots. He closes his eyes. His head spins. He lies back on the dirt as his forehead breaks out in sweat.

Later, Roberto opens his eyes.

*How long have I been asleep?*

He sits up.

*It cannot have been long. The sun is still high.*

He glances around, then up in the sky. The big, black birds are circling high.

*Every day they are there. Every day.*

He sits and stares at the dirt.

*Enough. This is enough. I cannot fight the desert. I hate this place.*

He picks up a couple of stones and throws them in disgust.

*No mas. No more. I am going home. I will find la migra. Let them take me. Either that, or I will die. I am never coming back to this place. Never.*

Roberto turns his head to the sound of a motor in the distance. A truck. He is sure of it. He crosses himself.

*The Virgin Guadalupe. She has saved me.*

His heart pounds. He stands, hoists the pack to his shoulder, then moves toward the road, slowly, step by step.

## Drops in the Desert

It is late April 2012 and I am with Ed McCullough and Al Enciso, volunteers with Tucson Samaritans, a group of humanitarian activists, many retirees, who put plastic one-gallon jugs of water in the desert where thirsty migrants might find them. For the past several hours we have been walking the length of Ramanote Canyon, a scruffy gash in the earth. The path follows the meandering and intermittent stream that feeds lush foliage, grass, and a few towering cottonwood trees. There are signs of recent use by migrants passing through. Empty cans of Red Bull, yogurt containers, plastic water bottles, and candy wrappers have been tossed by the wayside. The litter is not much, as far as migrant trails go, says Enciso. The more heavily used trails are trashed, unlike this one, which he thinks is used infrequently.

Ramanote Canyon empties into yet another, which we also walk before retracing our steps to one of the Samaritans' water drops near where we have parked. The half-dozen gallon containers of water, each marked with a date, have been untouched for the past month. McCullough and Enciso debate whether the spot should continue to be resupplied. There are other, better places that are more frequently used.

Picking and choosing water drop locations in the Arizona high desert, which might mean the difference between life and death for some migrants, is a hit-or-miss proposition. But McCullough has brought some scientific skill to it. An eighty-one-year-old retired chemist who has been involved in this humanitarian work since 2000, he has been mapping the migrant trails since 2004. He has traced our route on a GPS device that dangles from his neck. After each day's outing, McCullough adds the day's trail data to maps that he prints and keeps in a three-ring binder. The paths spread north from the Mexican border through some of America's most daunting terrain, tributaries of a human river flowing across the desert from the deep interior of Mexico and Central America.

McCullough creates his maps by tracking the movement of the water bottles. In addition to a date, each has a code noting where it was placed. When an empty container is found later, he knows where it was picked up, and by backtracking, he can trace a migrant trail. Lately the jugs have been moving southward, not northward, reversing the direction of the past decade. McCullough attributes this to the increased state and federal pressure on undocumented migrants to "self-deport." Many are leaving voluntarily.

The flight of migrants back to Mexico and Central America is a factor in the precipitous decline in apprehensions of undocumented migrants coming north, McCullough says, but it may not tell the whole story. "The Border Patrol says they catch most of the people [crossing the border]. But I don't think that's right. They have a very high presence. But the migrants have learned something, too. They've gotten smarter. Maybe more of them are getting through."

If the apprehensions are down, then the number of migrants found dead in the desert should also be down, McCullough says. But it's not. Based on data he has collected from the Pima County, Arizona, Forensic Science Center, which records recovered human remains for the region, the deaths in the desert are as high as ever. For the twelve months from October 2008 through September 2009, 189 human remains were found in the desert in Arizona's Pima and Santa Cruz Counties. During the subsequent twelve months in 2009–10, 224 remains were found. For that similar period in 2010–11, 177 remains were found. For the one-year span from October 2011 through September 2012, the remains of 171 people were found, a slight decrease.

From October 2012 to September 2013, however, 182 remains were found, indicating an upward trend.

"When we started coming out here in 2000, you would see people [crossing] every day," McCullough says. Estimates were that as many as two thousand people per day were crossing the border, which makes the official loss of migrant life in the borderlands rather paltry if less than two hundred die out of an estimated 730,000 crossings annually. The official number of migrant deaths may be low, he cautions, since "I think the number [of deaths] we have is a minimum" and many may remain in the desert undiscovered. "A lot of people die out there who no one knows about." McCullough adds that studies have shown that a corpse lasts just two weeks in the desert before it becomes a skeleton, because of animal scavengers and the arid climate. After that, only the bones remain, and the date and cause of death is forever obscure.

There is yet another explanation for the high number of dead turning up in the southern Arizona desert, McCullough says, an explanation that proves prophetic. The Border Patrol searches the area with helicopters, and pilots use a tactic called "dusting." They swoop down low over groups of migrants, scaring them with the deafening noise and thrashing wind. Rather than staying put, the group often scatters. Disconnected and disoriented, migrants become lost, run out of food and water, and possibly die. "It is all part of the strategy [to stem the flow of illegal immigration]," he says. "Scattering is making more people [become] lost."

The incidence of death in the desert may have also risen because of the increased number of Border Patrol checkpoints on main and back-country roads in the region, McCullough reasons. In the past, once migrants crossed the border, they would be met on backcountry roads by a van and taken to Tucson, Phoenix, or points beyond.

Now, with numerous checkpoints, most migrants must walk not just five or ten miles across the border, but as much as sixty miles north to Tucson, the first major community north of the border where they can blend into the general population. A young person who is in shape can make the trip in three days. But for some, it can take six days or more. "But you can't carry enough water for that," McCullough says. "It contributes to people dying."

Not everyone is happy with what the Samaritans do. "During the hot season, we get a lot of jugs slashed," McCullough says—anti-immigration groups are suspected—or "the Border Patrol will take them." Confrontations with the Border Patrol can be less than friendly. "We still run into Border Patrol who think that we're aiding felons. They think that because the migrants entered illegally, they deserve whatever happens to them. The government doesn't want to hear that we are saving lives."

Like most of the Samaritans, both Enciso and McCullough argue that illegal entry into the country is not a crime punishable by death. Once in the United States, people should be treated humanely, they say. "There comes a point in life when you can't let another person die out there because you did nothing," Enciso says as we trek along a dusty path to yet another water drop location.

A lot can be learned from what migrants leave along the trails, Enciso says. Many carry chunks of raw garlic to ward off rattlesnakes. Each migrant carries extra clothes for the cold nights in the high desert and supplies of food and water. Migrants drop their backpacks at pickup points when they're no longer needed.

As hundreds die in the desert, McCullough blames policy makers. Following the terrorist attacks of September 11, 2001, immigration and border security became the responsibility of the Department of Homeland Security. But terrorism has nothing to do with the immigration along the Mexican border, he says. The threat of terrorism has been used to mask rampant xenophobia that followed the attacks of 9/11. "The whole terrorism thing is a huge excuse to keep the Mexicans out. How many terrorists have we caught [on the US-Mexico border]?" he asks. "Zip."

McCullough makes a valid point. There is little readily available evidence that a clear "terrorist" threat exists along the US-Mexico border, an issue I will explore later in the book. The only notable exception involved the widely reported case of Mansour Arbabsiar, an

Iranian American used car salesman from Texas who was convicted of a plot to hire Mexican drug cartel killers to murder the Saudi Arabian ambassador to the United States. When Arbabsiar was arrested in September 2011, federal investigators said the plot involved members of Iran's Quds Force, a secretive wing of Iran's elite Islamic Revolutionary Guards Corps. In May 2013, Arbabsiar was sentenced to twenty-five years in prison.

Incidents of international terrorism are rarely mentioned in public debate about the US-Mexico border since few exist, yet the term "security" has become synonymous with the border and the *idea* of terrorism. The term "border security" has become a catchall phrase that includes immigration issues, drug and human trafficking, economic and social impacts of cross-border migration, and domestic and cross-border crime. What bothers McCullough so much is that with little evidence that terrorist organizations are using the US-Mexico border to infiltrate and threaten the United States, border security advocates rely on a handful of dramatic deaths and criminal incidents to inflate the "security threat" and to inflame antipathy toward immigrants, legal or not.

Our truck groans up a steep hillside on ranch land leased from the federal government. We have crossed numerous cattle guards, the frames of metal bars or pipes laid across the road and at fence lines because cattle will not cross them. The cattle guards were installed by the Border Patrol, McCullough says, because their ATV patrols were slowed when agents had to dismount to open and close gates in the fence lines.

Soon we are in a place called Lost Dog Canyon, a typically foreboding name given to the desert features hereabouts. As we crest the hill, a short and wiry man stands at the edge of the road. A black backpack sits in the dirt between his bent legs. He lifts a hand hesitantly, a gesture that is part wave and part appeal. McCullough stops. We climb out. Enciso, a native of Colombia, speaks Spanish to the man. "Do you have water?" Enciso asks.

The man nods.

"Do you have food?"

The man nods again.

This is Roberto, we learn, from Guatemala.

McCullough asks to see his water.

Roberto takes two bottles of brackish water from his pack.

"That's no good," McCullough says, and motions for Roberto to hand him the bottles. McCullough tosses them into the back of the truck, takes four bottles of fresh water from a plastic-wrapped package, and hands them to Roberto, who immediately twists off the top of one and gulps. "Do you have food?" McCullough asks again as Enciso translates.

"It's bad," Roberto says, and shows his mangled bag of Wonder Bread and the plastic bag of tortillas.

McCullough goes to the truck and returns with two small bags of protein bars, cookies, and plastic cups of applesauce.

"*Gracias,*" Roberto says with a nod, and explains that he came across the border four days ago with a group of fifteen people, some of them friends from Guatemala. They scattered when a helicopter swooped over them. Border Patrol agents captured six or seven, but the rest escaped. He has seen no one from the group since then and has been wandering the rugged hills alone for the past three days and nights. "I don't know where I'm going," Roberto says, squinting to the nearby hills, clearly disoriented.

McCullough and Enciso tell Roberto that he's not far from the border, less than ten miles, and can go back before he's caught.

Roberto shakes his head no. "I can't make it back by foot," he says. Even if he did go back, the return trip to Guatemala is long and difficult. "I don't have any money to travel," he says. Roberto crossed the border because there is no work in his hometown of Panajachel. He's handy with a shovel, he says, and makes a digging motion with his hands. He asks Enciso where New York is.

New York is a long way, too far for him now, Enciso says. "We're not far from Tucson." But Roberto has no idea where Tucson is, either. I am awed at this man's determination and can only imagine what desperation drives him. He has crossed much of the length of Central America in search of a dream, yet carries with him little sense of the daunting reality of his quest. He has no notion of where New York is yet is convinced, despite his slight frame, that his skill with a shovel and a good heart will see him through. This humble and harmless man constitutes the perceived threat against which America is spending billions of dollars annually and employing tens of thousands of armed personnel to secure the border. This diminutive, dehydrated, and frightened man is the focus of fearsome rage and enmity.

Roberto explains that he left his home at the edge of Lake Atitlan twenty-five days ago and has been on the road ever since. He paid a coyote, or guide, $1,300 to help him make the trip. Several in his group were middle-aged men who were so exhausted and their feet so sore that they couldn't walk and were captured. Now his money is gone and his spirit is broken. He has no choice but to return. "I want to go back," he says.

McCullough and Enciso ask if he is certain.

Roberto nods yes.

Roberto rests in the shade while we check on another water drop not far away, and when we return, he climbs into the back of the pickup and rides as we make the slow and bouncy trip back to the main roads. McCullough surmises that since Roberto was drinking from the fecal-laden water of the cattle pond, his dehydrated condition would have worsened rapidly if he had come down with dysentery, a common ailment suffered by migrants who refill empty jugs with water meant only for livestock. Roberto would have survived just a couple of days more, if that. It's one of the reasons that the Samaritans put clean water where migrants might find it.

McCullough parks on the shoulder when we reach the frontage road to Interstate 19, the road between the border town of Nogales and Tucson. He calls 911. McCullough explains to the dispatcher that Roberto has been wandering the desert for three days and may need medical care. While we wait, Roberto explains that he has a wife and three children in Panajachel. Though he can't read or write, he believes he had a chance for a new life in America.

Within ten minutes, a Santa Cruz County Sheriff's vehicle arrives and a deputy climbs out. The deputy is Hispanic and greets Roberto in Spanish, asking him some basic questions. Moments later, an emergency medical vehicle arrives. The deputy tells us that he picked up another migrant earlier in the day in much the same condition as Roberto—lost, disoriented, dehydrated, and asking to go home. The deputy assures McCullough that Roberto will be cared for while in his custody for the next couple of days, and then will be released to the Border Patrol. Typically, Roberto will be kept in federal detention with other Guatemalans until the immigration authorities have enough to fill an airplane to fly them back to Guatemala City. Before Roberto is led off to the medic, he shakes each of our hands, saying, "*Gracias, gracias.*"

We drive back to Tucson in silence, knowing that we probably violated Arizona's infamous anti–illegal immigration law, SB 1070. Under the original version of the law, it was illegal to transport anyone who might be suspected of being an illegal immigrant, for any reason, humanitarian or otherwise. Fortunately, McCullough explains, most local law enforcement people don't care and don't ask how or why you've got an illegal immigrant in your vehicle, especially if the person is being turned over to them. With the federal Border Patrol, it's different, he says, which is why he calls the local 911 first.

"We did a good thing today," McCullough says.

## Exposing Abuse

A day later I am in the Rincon Market deli in central Tucson with Leila Pine, a peace and immigrant rights activist. On the table is a seventy-two-page report titled *A Culture of Cruelty*, a project of No More Deaths, a group dedicated to stopping migrant deaths in the desert. Pine explains that the group began interviewing deportees about their treatment while in US immigration custody in 2006. Over the years, their stories have an accumulated weight that cannot be ignored. There are reports of routine physical and mental abuse, denial of needed medical care, denial of food and water. There are reports of gross over-crowding at the privately run detention centers, of unsanitary conditions, of extreme heat and cold.

The group's first report, titled *Crossing the Line*, was issued in 2008. It included hundreds of interviews of detained migrants at multiple locations along the border. The initial report revealed hundreds of incidents of abuse of migrants in US Border Patrol custody and called for standards and procedures for custody, as well as a mechanism for independent oversight.

No More Deaths continued the work and from the fall of 2008 to the spring of 2011 collected interviews with twelve thousand people, including men, women, and children, all of whom had spent time in Border Patrol custody. Subtitled *Abuse and Impunity in Short-Term U.S. Border Patrol Custody*, the 2011 report contained these conclusions:

* Only 20 percent of the people in custody for two or more days received a meal. Nearly all detainees said they were not given enough food.

* Water was denied to more than eight hundred people, and children were more likely than adults to be denied water, despite showing signs of dehydration.

* Ten percent of the detainees, or about twelve hundred people, including teens and children, reported incidents of physical abuse.

* Of the 433 reported cases in which medical care was needed, it was given in only 59 of the cases. That resulted in 374 cases of medical care being denied, or 86 percent of the total.

* Nearly half of those in custody, 5,763 people, reported overcrowded conditions, with about 25 percent, or 3,107 people, reporting unsanitary conditions.

* Nearly three thousand people said their personal belongings were not returned, including money in about two hundred of the cases.

* More than eight hundred people said they were deported separately from their family members.

* More than a thousand women said they were deported after dark, in violation of a Memorandum of Understanding between the Mexican Consulate and the US government.

Pine objects to deportees routinely being dumped on the Mexican border in the middle of the night. It's deadly dangerous for women and children. "There's nothing open. You have women and children alone. They can get raped and murdered." In some cases, the women have no idea where their husbands are since they've been held in and deported to different locations.

Pine has had her own encounters in the desert with the Border Patrol. While with a group distributing water bottles, she found herself surrounded by Border Patrol agents riding horses, driving SUVs, and hovering overhead in a helicopter. "They acted like they'd caught the largest dope-smuggling ring in the world," she laughs, albeit darkly.

One of the agents jumped off his horse and said, "You realize you're felons by aiding and abetting felons. You're tempting [migrants] to cross." When Pine's group showed no signs of leaving or stopping what they were doing, the agent warned, "I have more backup. It will be difficult for you." Pine says none of her group was deterred, but they were dismayed when agents slashed water bottles.

"We started out helping people coming north," she explains. "Now more and more, we're working with people who have just been deported."

Pine agonizes over some rare but troubling incidents. "We had two cases where Border Patrol agents kicked pregnant women sitting on the ground." The number of detainees who may have died in government detention facilities is unknown, she says, but Immigration and Customs Enforcement officials apparently admit to more than one hundred. Some people have been deported wearing only their underwear or a hospital gown, she says. "This is deliberate. It's not that they forgot their clothes."

The Border Patrol's response to the complaints from human rights activist groups is blunt, Pine says. "[The Border Patrol] wants this experience to be as bad as possible so [migrants] never try to do it again." The response has been equally insensitive from high levels in President Obama's administration, she says, which claims that the incidents of abuse are rare and amount to "collateral damage," since more than three hundred thousand people per year are deported.

The country needs a more humane and rational immigration and deportation policy, Pine argues, because immigration affects every community in America. "There is no city in the United States that does not have undocumented immigrants. They grow up thinking they're American. They don't speak Spanish and don't know a soul in Mexico. We deport them and they're terrified. The great majority of them have never committed crimes in their lives." Immigration policy with Mexicans is cruel and verging on illegal, Pine says. "This is systematic. It's coming from the top. We need systematic changes. This is a practice of severe human rights abuse. In some instances it rises to the level of torture."

## Militarized Border

The pervasive presence of the Border Patrol along the US-Mexico border seems to be a recent phenomenon, leading human rights groups and some longtime borderland residents to cry foul, but the contemporary militarization of the border can be traced back decades.

In 1989 President George H. W. Bush created Joint Task Force Six, a unit based at Fort Bliss in El Paso charged with helping local, state, and federal agencies fight the flow of illegal drugs across the borders of California, Arizona, New Mexico, and Texas. It was followed in 1993 by Operation Hold-the-Line, originally called Operation Blockade, which concentrated border agents in the El Paso area, and then Operation Gatekeeper, a President Bill Clinton initiative launched in September 1994 to stem the flow of Mexicans crossing the porous borders near San Diego, California. In 1997 Operation Rio Grande tried the same thing in southern Texas.

By 1995 Joint Task Force Six had become Joint Task Force North, and the drug-fighting expanded to cover all of the United States and its territories. Some five years later the task force was wrapped into the Department of Homeland Security and was told to combat "transnational threats." The US Army was now combating a domestic drug threat. Enlisting the army marked a policy change that categorized drug smuggling as an issue of national security.

Support for the military along the border has never been stronger. Look at the Border Security Enforcement Act of 2011, sponsored by former Republican presidential candidate Senator John McCain of Arizona.

The bill would have directed the secretary of defense to deploy at least six thousand members of the National Guard in the US-Mexico border region to help the Customs and Border Protection agency in "securing such border." This would have been a continuation of Operation Jump Start, the 2006 decision by President George W. Bush to send six thousand National Guardsmen to the borderlands while the US Border Patrol added thousands of agents. Jump Start ended in 2008 but was followed by Operation Phalanx in July 2010, ordered by President Obama and authorizing twelve hundred National Guardsmen also to back up the border control efforts.

McCain's bill also called for the federal courts to continue with Operation Streamline, its program to process captured migrants through the criminal justice system, and sought to reimburse local, state, and tribal law enforcement for migrant detentions. The Federal Emergency Management Agency was to beef up Operation Stone

Garden, money for local law enforcement agencies that helped control the border and detain undocumented migrants. There were brick-and-mortar projects, including permanent highway checkpoints; upgrades of the Border Patrol's "forward operating bases"; and completion of the seven hundred miles of border fence. A minor provision pointed to the small but unique problem that ultralight aircraft are used for smuggling drugs over the border.

The bill did not pass, but it reveals the range of programs already at play regarding border security. The US-Mexico borderland has become a militarized zone.

# 2

# A THOUSAND STORIES

✳

"**P***apelito, papelito,*" shouts **Father Peter Neeley,** as homeless migrants from the United States, Mexico, and Central America line the sidewalk outside El Comedor (the dining room).

It is 8:30 AM and the sun has begun to warm the day. I am several hundred yards inside Mexico, not far from the commercial port of entry on the US-Mexico border just west of Nogales, Sonora. These recently arrived deportees and migrants come to El Comedor to get a free meal, something they can do twice a day for up to ten days.

Wearing jeans, a blue polo shirt, and a straw cowboy hat and sporting a thick white beard, Neeley checks their *papelitos* (little papers). These slips of paper are stamped and dated immigration certificates vital to the deportees from the United States, since they mean not only meals for ten days but also a free bus ticket out of Nogales and to anywhere in the country, thanks to the government of Mexico. Deportees get the certificates moments after they're dumped at the border in downtown Nogales by US immigration authorities and then funneled into a Mexican immigration office. Neeley checks each certificate for the date, and with his nod, each eligible deportee or migrant climbs the concrete steps to the open-air meal center where posters proclaim that all people have the right to health, safety, employment, and respect.

El Comedor is a project of the Kino Border Initiative, a collaborative effort of various church groups spearheaded by the Catholic Church on both sides of the border. "People in Mexico don't have experience with shelters and soup kitchens because they don't exist here," explains Neeley. "This is a binational project. The women who volunteer here are from parishes in Mexico." The project is supported by volunteers and donated food. "We don't want to just write a check," he says, and so the program is based on activity, not passive giving.

A couple of Mexican federal police vehicles roll around the corner and park near the line of migrants. I look at Neeley, who shrugs. "This is to protect the migrants. The police are here because we asked them to be."

Most in line are deportees from the United States. The rest have arrived from central and southern Mexico, Guatemala, or Honduras with nothing but the clothes on their backs and without visas, passports, and money. Those from Central America have traveled for a month by train and by foot. They're vulnerable, Neeley says, not only to attacks and muggings but also to conscription by drug cartels that traffic them as contract labor into the United States or force them to carry drugs across the border.

Recruiters known as *enganchadores* prey on the migrants as they arrive and depart the kitchen, Neeley says. Sometimes the *enganchadores* infiltrate the migrants at El Comedor, then entice them with promises to take them across the border easily and cheaply. The recruiters work for the coyotes who arrange the crossings, and they collect a finder's fee for each person brought to a coyote. "It's a kind of kidnapping that they do," Neeley says. "They say they will take [deportees] across again."

Tightening the US-Mexico border has benefitted the drug cartels. "Now the drug dealers control the border and demand $100 to $200 to leave Mexico. This is all new," Neeley says, a practice that surfaced several years ago and has meant millions of dollars for the cartels.

By the time the chain-link door to El Comedor swings open at 9 AM each day, the line of deportees contains about eighty people, mostly men, and stretches down the block, nearly out of sight. The men clamber up the steps and slide onto long benches fronting wood and metal tables under a roof of corrugated metal.

Within minutes El Comedor is packed with hungry migrants sitting shoulder to shoulder. Before food is served, they stand, fingers locked in prayer as they recite Biblical passages led by the Sisters of the Eucharist. Neeley drapes a colorful piece of cloth around his neck and blesses the crowd. Soon plates of cooked eggs, rice, beans, vegetables, and tortillas are handed out of the tiny kitchen crammed with several cooks and volunteers. Pitchers of *horchata*, a drink of boiled rice and sugar, are poured into tall cups.

Today's El Comedor migrants are but a few of the hundreds and thousands of people caught in the crosshairs of the United States' beefed-up immigration enforcement. Their stories are fragments of broken dreams that clatter onto the tables.

Brought to America from Mexico by his parents at the age of three, sixteen-year-old Carlos Mota lived and attended school in Kansas for twelve years, completing his freshman year of high school. Mota's family owns land in Mexico, near the city of Veracruz on Mexico's eastern coast. Payments needed to be made or the government was going to reclaim the land, so the family went back to make good on the account. Mota's father, mother, and sister remained in Mexico, knowing how hard it would be to return to the United States. But Carlos wanted to go back, being more American than Mexican, he says, and to finish his high school education. His friends are in America. His life is there.

Carlos and a friend, who also wanted to enter the United States, contacted someone who could get them across the border. "We trusted him." The two young men got as far as Naco, Sonora, a tiny town on the border about sixty miles east of Nogales. They stayed several days and nights in a hotel waiting for the moment to cross the border. "We only ate ham sandwiches," Carlos says, until it was time to "make a hit," meaning go across. "It was not going to be hard, because all we had to do was jump the fence and hide in the grass."

It didn't turn out that way. The two friends had committed to paying their coyote $3,200 per person to get them across, a price that was due when they reached their destination. They had already paid members of the drug cartel that controlled that section of the border $150 each for the right to cross. "You have to pay so the mafia lets you cross the border," Carlos says, "and so they don't kill you." They then gave their coyote forty dollars to get them food and water that they would take across the border and moved into a position on the Mexican side of the border, waiting for their coyote to return with supplies. They sat in place nearly twelve hours, from 3 PM until 2 AM that night, growing hungry and thirsty. "It was starting to get cold. It started to rain," Carlos says. "We made a fire."

The coyote finally showed up with nothing but a few packages of sandwich meat. "Where is the rest of the food and money?" they asked. They were answered with a shrug. But they weren't in the mood to argue. They turned their attention to the US Border Patrol agents monitoring the section of the fence where they planned to cross. "When the rain came, they were not looking at us," Carlos says. "We tried to go between them," hoping that the darkness and the rain would provide cover.

"They saw us," Carlos says, and moments after he and his friend dropped off the fence and onto US soil, they were handcuffed and told to remove their shoelaces. "They took everything from us." They were put in a small van and taken to a detention facility. A few days later, they were bused to the border at Nogales in the middle of the night and released.

His meal finished, Carlos jumps up and says he has to go.

"But to where?" I ask.

Carlos shrugs, skips down the steps, and disappears.

## Trapped on the Border

I turn to a middle-aged man who has been listening intently to Carlos's story. He is Adelaydo Cornejo Hernandez, forty-six. He wears a sturdy canvas jacket and a baseball cap and has a thick beard of grey stubble. He looks at me with haunting grey-green eyes. He too had to pay *la mafia* $150 for the right to risk a border crossing.

The Mexican Army is aware of the fee but does nothing about it. "Why do you let the cartel do this?" Cornejo Hernandez had asked a soldier. The Mexican soldier responded by checking Cornejo Hernandez's backpack to make sure there were no drugs in it. "If you don't have any drugs, then you can try to cross," the soldier told him.

"What's the point of checking you for drugs?" I ask.

Cornejo Hernandez explains that the cartels have migrants carry large bundles of marijuana and other drugs across the border and don't want any migrants freelancing as mules for noncartel drug dealers. To get the drugs across successfully, they often distract the Border Patrol by sending migrants across knowing that they will be captured, and so divert the attention of the Border Patrol while others move the drugs across.

Cornejo Hernandez shakes his head in disgust, but there is nothing he can do. He's trapped and desperate to get back to his family in Santa Maria on California's central coast, where he arrived seventeen years ago and raised a family: a son, twenty-two; a second son, fourteen; and a daughter of seven. "I crossed the line looking for a job," he confesses. "I am a stonemason. Seventeen years ago, it was very different. There were fewer Border Patrol."

In addition to the masonry trade, Cornejo Hernandez worked in the rich agricultural fields in the region, now known for its vineyards. But the economic downturn of 2008 hit the migrant community hard. Jobs became scarce. Migrants came up short on rent and struggled to stay in the United States, he says.

A couple of months earlier, Cornejo Hernandez had gone to a party, drunk a few beers, then headed home about 8 PM. He was stopped by a local cop for a faulty taillight. Smelling beer, the officer gave Cornejo Hernandez a breath test, which he failed. He was fined $400 and spent the weekend in jail. "I got a lawyer," Cornejo Hernandez says, but as he tried to fight his fine and additional jail time for his DUI case, his file was handed over to the federal Immigration and Customs Enforcement (ICE) officials, who showed up at his court appearance. They asked where he was from. The Mexican state of Michoacán, he said, southwest of Mexico City.

Cornejo Hernandez was given two options: agree to voluntary deportation or hire an immigration lawyer at a cost of $4,000 to $5,000. "I signed the paper to leave," he says. On Thursday, April 5, 2012, he and other undocumented Mexicans were taken to Tijuana. The next day he got a ride to Nogales, a trip of 375 miles that took less than a day and where it was easy to cross back into the United States, he was told. He soon found a coyote willing to take him across.

There were six others in the group, and the coyote charged each $3,000. "When you get home, then you pay me," the coyote said. "Many people are watching for the Border Patrol and the helicopters," Cornejo Hernandez was told, yet "many, many people are making the crossing."

First stop was the Mexican Army. "The army checked my pack," Cornejo Hernandez says. "There were no drugs, only food." They let him and the others continue on. They began the crossing at 2 PM on a Friday, walking all day and night along the border, a trek of some forty miles to a spot near Sasabe, Arizona, a tiny border town where the Border Patrol is spread thin. Sasabe is adjacent to the sprawling Buenos Aires National Wildlife Refuge, one of the most heavily used areas for migrant crossings—one of which I will witness months later. The weather turned cold, Cornejo Hernandez says, rainy and damp, and he was not prepared for so much walking. "I got big blisters. I was tired." About 6 PM Saturday, as the sun was setting, they began to move again, one man at a time. "My feet were sore," he says. He was hobbling.

Out of nowhere, the Border Patrol appeared and the group scattered. Despite leg cramps, "I ran after my friends, but I stopped in some bushes," unable to continue. "I waited for a while." It was silent. "I didn't see my friends. I thought the coyote was coming [back] for me. I turned my head. I saw *la migra* [border agents]." One had a stun gun, he says.

Cornejo Hernandez was taken to a detention center in Tucson, where he was held for three days in a large cell that was so crowded that he could only stand. Food consisted of a small hamburger and a few cookies, he says. On the third night, Cornejo Hernandez was put on a bus. "There was just one on the bus, me." He was dropped off at the Nogales border crossing at 11 PM. He got his immigration certificate and spent the night on the streets of Nogales. The next morning, he made his way to El Comedor.

As we talk, Cornejo Hernandez's cell phone rings. He answers it briefly, talks, and hangs up, looking at me forlornly. It was a call from California, he says, from a former client who wanted to know if he could come do a job for him. He shrugs and shakes his head.

"What are you going to do?" I ask.

"I think I'll have a different plan. I need to talk to my son and wife. It's hard [to cross]. It's too hard. No more walking. It's too hard for me now." He points to his feet, which are bandaged and covered in clean white socks inside loose-fitting sandals.

Cornejo Hernandez plans to talk to the US consulate office in Nogales and begin the visa process. But before he can do that, he needs to get his DUI conviction off his record. "It's the only DUI I had in seventeen years. My record is clean."

He longs to be reunited with his family. His oldest son attended community college for two years and now works in a plant nursery. His younger son is in junior high school. Cornejo Hernandez is well aware of the legal complications he faces and acknowledges that he was in the country for nearly two decades without documents. But he had worked hard and had established a life and a family in the United States. "I'm in my country," he says of Mexico. "But it's hard on my daughter and sons."

Cornejo Hernandez's chances of being legally reunited with his family are slim. If it does happen legally, it will be a long and arduous process, one that possibly could take years. Under current rules, Cornejo Hernandez can claim that his separation creates a family hardship, and he can ask that the mandatory multiyear wait for a visa application be waived. If granted, he could return to the United States within a year. In 2011 immigration officials processed twenty-three thousand such waiver claims, and granted most of them. In the meantime, he must wait and survive.

## Honduras to Houston

Cornejo Hernandez turns to a young man sitting beside him, a twenty-one-year-old named Erlyn Fernando from Honduras. Cornejo Hernandez urges him to go back home. Fernando and a friend fled the poverty and escalating drug violence that has plagued their country as cartels have shifted operations into Guatemala and Honduras. The United States has responded by assigning Special Forces to assist those countries' drug police to combat the rising tide of drug violence there.

Fernando is married and has a young daughter, who is nearly three. Back home, he worked in restaurants, making only enough to survive. His town is controlled by gangs known as *maras* that engage in arms and drugs trafficking, extortion, human trafficking, gambling, kidnapping, money laundering, people smuggling, prostitution, racketeering, and robbery. Fernando says the *maras* force people to pay high rents, and if payment is late, they burn the house down.

"I'm looking for work to support my father and mother," Fernando says. "I can work as a cook or dishwasher." He has a brother in Houston, Texas, but his brother can't help him cross, he says, so he must cross on his own. Fernando made the journey to Nogales, as most others do from Central America, by climbing aboard a train and riding on top of a car with hundreds of others, crossing Guatemala and Mexico. He's been on the road for twenty-four days. "A lot of bad things happen on the trains," Fernando says. "They take our money. Sometimes they take us off the trains, and if you don't have money, they beat you."

Fernando was kidnapped for five days in Veracruz, a major Mexican city on the route from the south. Lacking money or papers, he feared for his life but was let go and now hopes to reach the United

States rather than return to Honduras. "I'm afraid to do that again," he says about traveling the length of Mexico on the immigrant trains, explaining that his best friend died on the trip north.

Fernando is desperate. He has yet to attempt the border crossing, because he lacks the money to pay a coyote. Yet he can't stay in Mexico, since he also lacks the documents that would allow him to work here. His ten days of free meals at El Comedor are finished. "I don't know where I will stay. Now there is hardly any work and there are bandits. You don't know who to trust."

"What are you going to do?" I ask.

"We have to look for work. It is the only way to get ahead. We may try to cross today. If we don't, we will try to get some work here."

## Triage

Not far from El Comedor and only a few blocks deeper into Nogales, migrants get free medical care and access to free telephones. The clinic and call center are operated by the Kino Border Initiative inside the compound of Grupo Beta, a Mexican police unit that began operations in Tijuana in 1990 to protect northbound migrants from criminals and has evolved into an agency of the Mexican immigration service.

The deportees from the United States and migrants on their way north arrive here with blisters and sprained ankles and are often dehydrated. During the wet winters, they arrive with colds, the flu, and wet, sore feet. "Some [deportees] get medical care" while in US immigration custody, says Sarah Roberts, a volunteer with No More Deaths and a registered nurse from Tucson, "but many don't. We've been advocating for more medical services at the clinic. This is sort of a triage service." Roberts helps at the clinic, where from fifteen to eighteen people per day are treated for various health problems, she says.

The clinic hands out what Roberts calls "harm protection kits," clear plastic bags with vials of just enough bleach to purify a bucket of stream water, electrolyte tablets, charcoal water filters, and ointments. "People tell us that it's saved their lives," she says.

Physical ailments are not the only problems. Norma Quijada, the Mexican nursing coordinator for the Kino clinic, explains that "some are at the point of wanting to commit suicide. I feel I have to talk to them for a long time. It scares me to think they might do something to themselves. It's a part of my job that is not easy."

Women who attempt to cross the border are extremely vulnerable, Quijada says. "The coyotes do terrible things to the women. We try to warn pregnant women about how dangerous it is." But some are desperate. "They want to join husbands and family," she says.

Across the compound is another volunteer, Samara Rosenberg, twenty-seven, of Pittsburgh, who helps migrants use the free telephones to contact family and friends. It can be a life-saving call, she says, enabling money to be wired to help the deportees and migrants survive and get back home. "A guy arrived here who had been in the United States for forty years," she says. "He had no connections to Mexico."

Free phone calls are often not enough. Deportees have been stripped of their identification, Rosenberg says, which prevents them from collecting money at Western Union offices. They're alone and penniless. "It can be really dangerous for people who have never been [in Mexico]. It's a shame for them to be deported to a strange place and have no idea where their family and friends are. That's a human rights abuse. We hear reports of physical abuse by the Border Patrol and a lack of food, water, and medical care. There's overcrowding in the jails. All those things are going on. We're trying to reduce the harm caused by deportation," she says.

## Desperate Crossings

Across the street from the El Comedor kitchen and up a steep hill is an apartment complex where the Kino Border Initiative maintains several apartments, one of which is a shelter for women and children. It is here where I meet Marla Conrad, a social worker and graduate student researching gender-based violence along the border. "We see

hundreds of women per year. A lot of the women will pair up to protect each other." It's a matter of survival. In one recent case, she says, a
man offered a soda to a woman who was traveling alone and waiting
at a bus station. The man warned her to be careful in the town. She
took a couple of sips, then woke up later that night nearly half naked
and in an alley. The soda had been laced with a drug and she'd been
raped.

Women face serious dangers when they cross the border, even as
part of larger groups, Conrad says. Women are assaulted by the coyotes
who guide groups across the border. "The risk is with the people [who
are] crossing them." If women don't submit to the sexual demands of
the guides, "they are left behind." Women acquiesce to sexual assault
so they're not abandoned, Conrad says. One case involved a woman
who was eight months pregnant and refused to have sex with a guide.
She was left behind and wandered four days before being picked up by
the Border Patrol.

The coyotes are not the only problem. On the Mexican side, the
migrants are also subject to attacks by the cartel members and their
enforcers, known as *sicarios*, or assassins. If the migrants don't pay the
crossing "tax" they can be kidnapped, the women raped and held for
ransom. There are also desert bandits, the *bajadores*, who rob and rape.

"Why do women take such risks?" I ask.

Conrad sighs and shakes her head. "Violence and corruption push
people to the United States. They're looking for a safe place to live and
make some money." Despite the dangers and the deportations, they go
back. "After experiencing the worst, they keep trying."

At the Kino shelter that day is Guille Gonzales, an energetic Mexican woman and mother of five who worked for many years as a
housekeeper and maid in Phoenix. She has been traveling with her
two daughters, Yazmin, seventeen, and Brenda, fourteen, and her
eleven-year-old son, Giovanny. She's determined to get across the border to Phoenix, where she plans to pick up her youngest daughter, an
American citizen, who crossed into the United States earlier in the
year and is staying with relatives. She then plans to continue on to

Albuquerque, New Mexico, where she wants to join her oldest son, a nineteen-year-old.

Gonzales sits at the dining room table of the Kino shelter surrounded by her family. The shelter is quiet and clean, with a small kitchen and several bedrooms with bunk beds and clean linens. Crosses and religious pictures adorn the walls. When Arizona's notorious immigration law SB 1070 was passed, Gonzales said she grew increasingly afraid that her children would be taken or that she'd be sent to Mexico and permanently separated from them. So she fled Phoenix, taking her children to her family home in Puebla, a sprawling city of about two million people seventy miles southeast of Mexico City. But jobs were scarce, she says, and after a year of struggle, she decided to return to the United States.

She got as far as the town of Altar, about sixty miles south of the US border, where she made contact with a coyote who agreed to take her and her family across. They decided to risk the crossing despite the dangers, since they knew and trusted the coyote. He was charging them $2,000 per person, a total of $10,000 for all. The money would be paid back in installments when Gonzales found work.

They made their way to the border, where they spent two days and nights on the Mexican side waiting to cross because of the Border Patrol presence. The family was part of a group of thirty-four people. It was cold and damp, and each night they slept in the open, protected from the chilling rains by plastic tarps. At night they huddled around small campfires. When the daytime temperature soared, the group rested in the shade of spindly mesquite bushes.

In the middle of the afternoon on the third day, they began to walk. To avoid detection, they walked the most rugged terrain, Gonzales says, going up and over two small mountains. Some slopes were so steep that they had to climb using their hands and feet and slide down the other side. Every few hours, they took a break. "Everybody helped each other." But the trek continued relentlessly. "We were sleeping under trees in the mountains. We walked all day and night."

On the third night, the group was awakened by the ominous thudding of a Border Patrol helicopter. It swooped overhead, then turned and shined a powerful spotlight on the migrants. Four Border Patrol officers appeared. "They said, 'Don't move.' But others tried to run. They got them and they hit them." One young woman was grabbed, Gonzales says, pushed to the ground. A Border Patrol officer put his knee on her mouth to keep her down, even though the young woman was not struggling. "They used the f-word. Everyone was captured."

The migrants were handcuffed together and walked for two more hours to a road, Gonzales says, where they encountered about ten Border Patrol trucks. After removing their shoelaces and having their backpacks emptied of food, they were loaded into the trucks. The family was taken to a detention facility in Casa Grande, Arizona.

The facility provided two gallons of drinking water for twenty-five people, Gonzales says, and the toilet had no door. They slept three days on the floor with only a blanket. Conditions worsened at a holding facility in Tucson. "They didn't let us sleep. We had to stand up all the time. It is worse for the men. In a room meant for forty, they put eighty. In the United States, they treat immigrants worse than animals. They say they respect human rights," Gonzales says with a cynical laugh.

Authorities took the family to the Nogales border crossing late at night. Gonzales and her children found their way to the Kino shelter, where they have been living for a week.

"What is your next move?" I ask. "Are you going back to Puebla?"

Gonzales shakes her head. "We're waiting to cross again."

Gonzales is desperate enough to risk another crossing. She acknowledges that what she is doing is illegal but knows that many people do it every week. "Each person has a [reason] and they're willing to risk [losing it all] to do it again and again," she says.

"What is the solution to the immigration problem?" I ask.

Gonzales thinks for a moment. "I was thinking about how much money they spend for immigration enforcement. Why don't they put money into more visas? Most people want to be able to return to Mexico. But what they do now is no good. They treat people like animals."

## Right from Wrong

Later that day I walk with Father Neeley along the streets of Nogales, Sonora. This once thriving and colorful border town is dying. Two-thirds of the shops and restaurants that once catered to swarms of American tourists are boarded up. The few shopkeepers and restaurateurs who remain now bark at passersby, directing them into the darkened interiors, saying, "What would you like? You want to get high? How about a woman?"

Neeley directs me down a side street and around a corner where we encounter the wall that splits the city and divides the two countries, a wall that until a few years ago did not exist. Inside the city, it's an architecturally acceptable wall of stucco and painted metal grating. But a couple of blocks in either direction, it becomes a tall barrier of rusted steel bollards, a rebirth of the Cold War's Iron Curtain that separated east and west Berlin.

We pause at a boarded-up hotel that Neeley says was purchased by a drug cartel. A tunnel was dug from the hotel and under the fence to the American side, easing the movement of drugs and people into the United States. It was discovered and closed.

We take a seat in a restaurant patronized by Nogales residents and businessmen. Over lunch, Neeley complains about US immigration law and border policy, which he describes as "draconian" because it ignores the human impact of bureaucracy. "It's hard to separate all of this [policy] from the human beings. Lives are being affected," and not in good ways. Policy makers need to "go to the desert to see all of those who died due to [decisions] made in Washington, DC. No one in their right mind would cross the border in the desert. But desperate people are not thinking clearly. There is a human cost to the immigration policy."

Human smuggling across the border has always been a problem, but worsened as the Border Patrol expanded exponentially. Until 2006 smuggling was a "mom and pop" operation. "Then the cartels moved in and found that it's as lucrative to run people as it is drugs," Neeley says, and now, too many people are suffering needlessly.

"What do you say when people accuse you and the humanitarian groups such as the Samaritans and No More Deaths of aiding and abetting migrants to break the law?" I ask.

Neeley looks at me. "We're not talking about legal or illegal," he says. "We're talking about what's right or wrong."

## The American Andes

Several months later, I am in Denver and talking with a migrant whom I'll call Ernesto because he fears being found by immigration authorities. Ernesto is from the state of Nayarit in Mexico and lives with his wife, young son, and his wife's nephew, also from Mexico. Ernesto works in the kitchen of an Indian food restaurant in southwest Denver, not far from his small, sparely furnished apartment. He first came to the United States as part of an agricultural H 2A visa program that provides sheepherders for the remote sheep and cattle ranches in northwestern Colorado, eastern Utah, and southwestern Wyoming.

Although the daily realities of the sheepherders may be difficult, the program is an example of how immigrant labor fills a critical need in the US economy while providing income for workers from abroad who desperately want the money. The herders return home once their three-year contracts are complete, reconnecting with families, friends, and relatives. Some, however, use their legal visa as an opportunity to escape what they view as low pay and bad working conditions and fade into the larger illegal immigrant community that numbers about twelve million people, who toil in the shadows of the US economy.

Ernesto first came in 2010 after signing a contract to work on one of the Colorado ranches for $750 per month. After complaining to his bosses, he says, he was provided with a horse so he would not have to herd the sheep on foot. However, Ernesto was thrown from the horse and injured his leg, shoulder, and face. When the rancher told Ernesto there was no time to take him to the hospital since he was so far into the mountains, Ernesto left his job and made his way to Denver, where he found work in a restaurant kitchen. He has no intentions of going back to Mexico, he says, because there is "a better life here" and the cost of paying a coyote to come back across the border is too high. The memory of his time in the mountains lingers, however. "When it gets cold, my shoulder hurts," he says, and he has pain in his face. Ernesto plans to stay in the United States for at least ten years or until his son is educated.

Ernesto is one of a number of herders whom I encounter on a trip to western Colorado in the fall of 2012, most of whom are from Peru or Bolivia. Although the visa program provides legitimate employment for about fifteen hundred herders from Central and South America arranged through two nationwide ranching associations, the program has critics.

"This is like human trafficking," says Ricardo Perez, director of the Hispanic Affairs Project of Montrose, Colorado. "It's like being in jail. You can't leave." Most herders are from South America, and upon arrival in the United States are taken by their ranchers directly into the mountains, where they remain for months at a time. Once their multiyear contracts end, they are flown back to South America. "The industry prefers South American workers [to Mexicans] because they can't go home easily," Perez says.

In October 2012 Perez and I travel to a dusty mountain camp to meet a few herders. They have gathered their flocks and are preparing to take the sheep to lower elevations for the approaching winter. Perez explains that ranchers do as little as is necessary for the herders. "If there are any improvements [to conditions], it is because the herders take some action," such as contacting activists or lawyers at Colorado Legal Services, which at this writing has a federal suit pending against at least one sheep rancher.

As we sit in one of the *campitos*, the cozy portable trailers in which the herders live, and share a meal of roast mutton, Perez and I talk with a sheepherder whom I'll call Diego, which is not his real name, who is from a community near the Bolivian capital of La Paz. The son of a tin miner, Diego graduated from high school. When he saw how people were being exploited in the tin mines, he vowed that "I couldn't live the life of my father." He moved to La Paz, where he worked a variety of low-paid, unskilled jobs. "I worked at everything, but I don't know anything in depth," Diego confides.

When he heard that sheepherders, called *pastores* in Spanish, were being recruited to work in the United States, he applied. The jobs are competitive, Diego says, because the recruiters want herders who are likely to stay despite the remote and rigorous conditions they must face. The *pastores* are screened through a series of interviews. "They prefer someone who has never been outside of their village and who is illiterate. We came here without any idea what it was like," Diego says of his compadres. "You hear of many jumping ship."

At first Diego didn't know how to interact with the ranchers. "There is intensive control of our activities." Ranchers keep their visas, he says, and justify that by saying, "the *campitos* can catch fire." The ranchers frequently ask, "Has anyone visited?" Diego says. "They try to keep us isolated. They say, 'There are lots of dangerous people [around].'" The ranchers tell the herders, "Ask me for things, not other people."

Loneliness is a problem. "Sometimes we cry," Diego says. When he talks to his nine-year-old son on the telephone, his son cries. "It's hard. The bosses only care about the well-being of their animals." The loneliness is made worse by the lack of contact herders have with other people. "When people talk to us like individuals, it is startling," Diego says. "We thought all Americans were [rude]. Some people look at us like we're a strange animal. It begins to affect you. You become a hermit and don't like people. When you are done for the day, you don't feel like eating. Little problems become distorted because you think about them all the time. It is important to have a contact with the outside world. Your self-esteem and self-worth are at stake."

The first time Diego came to the United States as a herder, he didn't have access to a cell phone. But conditions have improved. "Things change. Certain [ranchers] pay workers better. If conditions were improved, [more] people would be willing to work at this job," Diego says. "If the conditions were better, I wouldn't ask myself why I'm here." One of the herders' biggest complaints is the lack of time off, since sheep need to be tended round the clock. In Bolivia it is traditional to take Sundays off, he says, but not in the United States. "I understand I'm here to work. It's a job."

After extended periods of time away from his family, friends, and community, "returning home is a shock," Diego says. "Friends are gone. Things have changed. According to law, we have to go back. What we miss [is] friends and family."

Because one herder, whom I call Raoul, never had a horse, he was on foot and so exhausted at the end of the day, he rarely felt like eating. "After a day like that," says Raoul, "I'd fall asleep without eating. The [boss] only came to chew me out," then asked him, "Why are you complaining? This is paradise."

Timely pay can be a problem, Raoul claims, and had heard of a rancher who withheld pay for a year or more, claiming he was broke. "We didn't know where to go or what to do" in such cases, Diego says. Herders are paid on the last day of their contract to keep herders in line, Diego says. "Pay at the last minute is a way to keep them under control."

When the job is finished, they're taken directly to the airport, Raoul says, adding, "I have worked on the day I was leaving," and remembers finishing a job at 10 AM and being taken immediately to an airport for a 2:30 PM flight that day.

This can be followed by a wait of two or three months for their accumulated pay to be wired, Diego explains. The employment contracts specify conditions, but no one enforces the provisions, such as time off and vacation pay, Diego says. "The contract is hard to understand. Only if you say you're going to find another job at another ranch will they do something." The herders must contact one of the two ranching associations to register complaints before conditions and requests are met, he says.

Raoul tells of a friend who asked to be transferred to a new ranch, and instead was sent back to Bolivia, even though he wanted to keep working. The rancher took $600 out of his wages for sodas and other items and then made the herder pay his own airfare back to Bolivia.

Such practices have been noted in a January 2010 report titled *Overworked and Underpaid*, prepared by the Migrant Farm Worker Division of Colorado Legal Services. The report concludes that herders "suffer many indignities because of the lack of sufficient standards in place concerning their working conditions."

Included in the report is a photocopied pay statement for a herder, dated April 2008. The herder was to be paid $750 for the month's wages, but after a variety of expenses were deducted, he ended up with just $88.40. The deductions included: $185 for the first of six reimbursement payments to the rancher for the herder's airfare to the United States; $80 for raingear; $42 for boots; $52 for binoculars; and $28 for a belt, camera, and alarm clock.

The report was based on research by Spanish professor Thomas Acker of Colorado Mesa University in Grand Junction, who interviewed ninety-three herders in western Colorado from December 2007 to December 2009. The report recommends a range of improvements for the working conditions of the herders, including wages that equate to those of farm workers, mandatory annual inspections by federal agents from the Department of Labor, access to running water and toilets, regular time off, off-ranch visits, and access to telephones or personal cell phones.

## Friend to the Herders

One of those helping the herders is Juan Chumacero Sr., who moved to the small ranch town of Rangely in northwestern Colorado in the late 1990s after retiring in California. "I used to go visit them every week," Chumacero says of herders in his community. He gave herders things that the ranchers didn't, such as fresh fruit, sodas, and cooked food. If Chumacero had been fishing, he'd take fresh trout and cook it for them, he says.

When herders said they had no way to call home, Chumacero brought them prepaid cell phones. "You call me when you need something," he said. "Now a lot of them do have phones." But he adds, "If the ranchers find out who they're calling [to complain about conditions], then they get reprimanded."

Reprimands were not Chumacero's only worry. "My concern is their medical attention. I take them aspirin. The ranchers take care of them to a certain point, [such as] when they have accidents. Otherwise, nobody pays attention to them. We buy bars of soap and toothpaste and laundry soap. We take that stuff to them. But if they forget to hide it, the bosses want to know where they got it. They get angry. They're afraid they might leave the sheep. Some [herders] do leave. They become outlaws. That's what they call them. [Herders] get serious when I'm talking with them. They're scared."

In the mid-1960s, Chumacero says, herders were recruited from all over the world but were offered a chance for citizenship through their work. "In those days, they came with five-year visas. Then after the five years, they could stay here. But today, they can't, and they don't want to. They miss their families and want to go back."

Chumacero recalls meeting a Peruvian herder named Anselmo. "I went to Anselmo one day and asked where his horse was. He said, 'I don't have a horse.' There was snow on the ground, and he had to trudge through the snow to find the sheep." The rancher had told the Peruvian, "You're used to walking, so walk." When Chumacero complained to the county sheriff about Anselmo's treatment, the sheriff called the rancher. "Two days later, he had a horse."

After decades of helping the herders, Chumacero continues his mission. "I usually go meet them in the evenings when the bosses won't be around. I don't want the bosses to take it out on them. It's not right. Everybody here has a right to talk to people. [Herders] sometimes ask me to send their money [to] Peru. I then call the families to tell them to pick it up."

Chumacero has had confrontations with ranchers. When a ranch boss didn't take a herder firewood and fresh water, the herder called Chumacero, who drove to the young man's camp with food and other supplies. Later the same day, the herder called Chumacero again, saying that he had been fired when the ranch boss saw the food and supplies. Fearing for the young herder's safety, Chumacero called the county sheriff. "I told the herder, go to the road," he says, where the sheriff met him. But the herder called Chumacero yet again, saying that now the ranch boss and a ranch hand were not letting him leave. "They want me to go, but they won't let me leave the camp," the herder said.

"The ranch hands were laughing," Chumacero says with disgust. "It was a joke to them." But it wasn't funny. "All he was going to do was eat some baked chicken." Chumacero took the herder home, fearing that if he had been left alone, "they would have beaten the crap out of him and dumped him somewhere. I took the boy to Meeker and he left. That's the stuff they go through all the time."

## Ranchers Respond

The Colorado Legal Services report detailing abuses of the South American sheepherders generated an outcry from Colorado sheep ranchers, who accused the report's drafters and researcher of distorting the facts and intentionally generating an anti-ranching bias. In a March 12, 2010, response by the Colorado Wool Growers Association, Executive Director Bonnie Brown challenged the CLS study, saying, "Sheep herding on the open range can be a lonely and difficult job; however, isolated and sometimes challenging working conditions do not equate to abuse." Brown explained that almost all of the sheepherders in Colorado are brought to the state either through the Western Range Association (WRA) or Mountain Plains Agricultural

Service (MPAS), and that "these organizations are readily available to help resolve conflicts between workers and employers."

The WRA membership consists of 218 sheep ranchers, and MPAS has 264 sheep and cattle ranchers, all of whom participate in the foreign herders program. The two groups employ from fifteen hundred to two thousand herders at any given time. The sheep ranchers are sensitive to criticism, because the lamb and wool business is a $1-billion-per-year enterprise, according to the WRA. The two groups reportedly account for about 60 percent of the lamb and wool produced in the United States. Employment of foreign herders began in the 1950s, when few US workers would take the job. Without the foreign herders program, the industry could face ruin, the association says.

Brown disputed the complaints that ranchers withhold worker visas and that herders do not understand their contracts, saying those practices are illegal. "Employers would . . . run afoul of federal laws, policies and regulations," she said, if they worked that way. The herders are briefed on the details of their contracts "in Spanish before they leave their home country," and again when they arrive in the United States prior to signing it.

Many of the abuses revealed in the CLS report appear to have been addressed officially, at least, through the US Department of Labor's recent requirements regarding the herders. According to the department's Training and Employment Guidance Letter dated June 14, 2011, ranchers must provide the herders with "sufficient housing . . . at no cost"; workers' compensation insurance; "an effective means of communicating" with their bosses in case of emergencies, such as satellite phones, cell phones, or radios; three meals a day or "free and convenient" food and cooking facilities; and monthly or semimonthly pay with "accurate and adequate records."

Brown also disputed the complaints about poor herder pay, pointing to a February 2010 analysis prepared for the association by consultant Julie Stepanek Shiflett of Collbran, Colorado, titled *The Real Wage Benefits Provided to H-2A Sheep Herders and the Economic Cost to Colorado Ranchers*. Shiflett concluded that with food and housing benefits, a herder's $750 per month pay is the equivalent of $1,638 per month, or more than $10 per hour.

Brown noted that the South American sheepherders participate in the program because they earn good wages compared to what is available in their home countries. Most herders have accepted multiple contracts and have worked an average of seven and a half years in the program, according to a survey of more than 90 percent of the Colorado sheep ranchers, each of whom employ about five herders per ranch. "H2A sheep herders choose to participate in this program," Brown said. "If the program was rife with abuse, neglect, and mismanagement, herders would not continue to participate."

Ranchers who employ the herders acknowledged in a video documentary produced by the Colorado Wool Growers Association (www.coloradosheep.org) that some abuses may have occurred, but they are few and far between. Meeker, Colorado, sheep rancher Angelo Theos explained in the video that it is in a rancher's best interests to keep the foreign sheepherders happy. "If they're not content . . . they won't do a good job with livestock."

Steve Kreis, a Montrose, Colorado, nondenominational missionary with the organization InFaith, has ministered to the herders for eleven years. He said in the video that "there is not a perfect world here. Both sides have their problems. And both sides have their blessings. All of us would like to see [the program] better for everybody. There are problems, but that does not mean abuse."

## Their Jobs Are Waiting

In early November 2012 I cross into Agua Prieta, Sonora, and make my way to the office of Ricardo Moreno, the coordinator for Centro de Atención al Migrante Exodus, a migrant aid center. Supported by Catholic Relief Services and bolstered by donations of clothes and by volunteers from the Presbyterian border ministry Frontera de Cristo, the center is comparable to El Comedor, the kitchen in Nogales, Sonora. In addition to offering migrants two meals a day, this center provides overnight accommodations for migrants who find themselves stranded in Agua Prieta either on their way to the United States or having been deported.

Heightened border security by the United States has not slowed the waves of migrants waiting to cross, Moreno says. In the first three months of the year, the center fed and housed fifteen hundred migrants, nearly double the number of migrants they housed and fed for the same time period the year before. By early November 2012 the center had hosted thirty-five hundred, well more than the average of past years. About 70 percent of those traveling to the United States are going for work, Moreno says, and the remaining 30 percent want to reunite with family members there.

Migrants have a strong moral as well as economic incentive to cross the border, Moreno says. Mexico's minimum wage is about $4.25 per day. "There is work in Mexico, but the pay is not just," he says. "The government of Mexico does little to help people, especially along the border." Since migrants can earn much per hour in the United States, they believe they have a moral obligation to cross the border to help their families. They make the crossing despite the payment demanded by the coyotes, up to $4,000, to make the trip. Some also endure extortion once they're in the United States and working, he says.

Moreno believes that the US government deports people because the economy has declined and jobs are scarce. "I feel there is not a lot of work in the US. That is why not a lot of people are allowed to cross legally. If there is a need for labor there, the border crossing would become easier. It's a function of how much work there is. That is why fewer people are crossing, not stricter enforcement."

After the center's evening meal is served in a small dining hall with about twenty-five people, I sit down with two young Mexicans, Luis, twenty-four, and his girlfriend, Carolina, twenty-five, both of whom are from Mexico City. Both have worked in the United States, Luis since 2005 and Carolina since 2008, and both went back to Mexico hoping to reestablish themselves. But jobs were scarce, so they decided to return to the United States. Their first attempt to cross the border failed after they paid a coyote only about $110 each. Rather than taking them across the border, the man turned them over to US immigration authorities.

Carolina and Luis say they have jobs waiting for them. Luis worked as a plumber in Fort Myers, Florida, at a complex of beachfront rental units, making nineteen dollars per hour. He learned plumbing at the age of seventeen while working with his father in Mexico City. Luis first crossed the border in 2005, hooking up with relatives living and working in Indianapolis, Indiana. He heard of good-paying jobs in Florida, so he left and found work there as a plumber.

Carolina worked in a bar that caters to the Mexican community in Fort Myers, she says, and expects to get her old job as soon as she returns. Carolina first traveled to the United States in 2008, crossing near Agua Prieta and stopping in Phoenix before continuing on to New Jersey, where she worked for three months. She went to Florida as well after hearing about work in Fort Myers, where she met Luis. "I'm not afraid because I crossed once before," she says.

Luis and Carolina have contacted a more reliable coyote for their next try. It will cost them $3,900 each. They must pay half of the cost when they reach Phoenix and the rest when they reach Fort Myers. Their family will help them make the hefty payments, they say. Neither is shocked at the cost, and both say that the risk is worth it. "There are some coyotes who are bad and there are some migrants who are bad and run away without paying," Luis says.

With so many people crossing the border so easily, and with so many waiting to do so, I need to know more about what is being done to secure the border. I go to El Paso to find out.

# II

★ ★ ★

# THE BUSINESS OF FEAR

# 3

# THE FRONTIER OF FEAR

✳

**O**ctober 2012, El Paso, Texas. Opening day of the annual Border Management Conference and Technology Expo, where purveyors of high-tech security and surveillance systems peddle their aerial detection systems, ground sensors, and armored and robotic vehicles to the US Customs and Border Protection (CBP) agency. These merchants of border security ply their products in a machismo-charged atmosphere where the ethos is pure: stop a threat to America that did not exist a decade ago.

Immigration and border control is no longer a process by which agents monitor and regulate the flow of people and products across a border that for hundreds of years has been relatively open, marked mostly by stretches of barbed wire fences intended to keep cattle from wandering to and from neighboring Mexican ranches. Today it's an us-against-them mind-set that arose from the smoldering ruins of September 11, 2001. But the terrorist threat from America's southern border is more fear than fact.

Fear is fact, however, just a short distance from the expo in Juárez, Mexico, which sprawls along the other side of the meandering and muddy Rio Grande and is perhaps the deadliest city in the world. Once a thriving metropolis where for decades Americans indulged in vices, Juárez has become a graveyard, ground zero of the cartel wars, creating a petrified populace. The shadow of death that hovers over Juárez extends across the river, lending a sense of urgency to this exposition aimed at averting an apparent Mexican migrant apocalypse.

From 2008 to 2012 some 10,500 people were killed on the streets of Juárez, mostly the foot soldiers of drug and crime cartels. The Juárez–El Paso region is a major gateway from Mexico into the United States for an array of manufactured goods and food products, as well as drugs. Control of such transit points, known as *plazas* in the drug cartel parlance, is big business. Each *plaza* is valued in the tens of billions of dollars per year.

The killing in Juárez peaked in 2010, when the city had a staggering 3,115 homicides, with some months marked by more than 300 deaths. The annual death toll in Juárez, with an estimated population of 1.6 million people, was ten times that of Detroit, considered one of the deadliest cities in the United States. With a population of 700,000, less than half of Juárez, Detroit had 309 homicides in 2010. In 2011 Detroit counted 344 murders, and in 2012 it logged 411 homicides, according to crime statistics. More comparable is Chicago with a population of more than 2.7 million, which in 2012 recorded a record 506 homicides. As in Juárez, the Chicago murders have been linked to internecine gang violence and the Mexican drug cartels.

In stark contrast to the death rate in Juárez is the low death rate in El Paso, just across the border. With a population of about 650,000, El Paso was touted in 2010 as being among the safest cities of its size in the United States, with only five murders that year. In 2011 that number increased to sixteen.

To say that Juárez is a war zone is an understatement. The four-year death toll for Juárez exceeds US military fatalities in the Iraq and Afghanistan wars, about five thousand and two thousand respectively. If one looks at all of Mexico, estimates are that from fifty thousand to seventy thousand people have died during a decade of drug-related violence. In late December 2012 the Associated Press reported that this figure may be low, because it does not include the more than twenty thousand people who have simply disappeared, says a Mexican group called Propuesta Cívica, or Civic Proposal. Adding the number of disappeared pushes the total Mexican human carnage to about ninety thousand deaths from 2006 to 2012. Such a number compares to the *civilian* casualties of the US wars in Iraq and Afghanistan. According to various sources, civilian deaths in the eight-year Iraq war were between 110,000 and 120,000, while civilian deaths in Afghanistan are estimated to be about 12,700 for the past decade.

No one here at the expo, however, bothers to talk about the deeper realities of why this conference has come into existence, the causes of the carnage across the river, how these causes might be addressed, or what is driving the torrent of humanity across the US-Mexico border. Instead, talk is of things that fly and hang in the sky and will hopefully prevent Mexico's problems from spilling across the border.

## Day of the Drones

Unmanned Aerial Systems Focus Day opens the expo and is all about drones and helium-filled balloons called aerostats that are tethered to the ground by cables and relay data from highly sensitive cameras and devices that can find and follow virtually anything that moves on the ground, day or night.

Aerostats are all over Afghanistan, and I'd seen them when I was there throughout 2010 and 2011 as they floated over Kabul and many other locales across the country. Aerostats give US forces a 24-7 eye in the sky and are highly useful devices, warning of impending attacks and targeting enemy operatives. In the eastern Afghan city of Jalalabad, a Predator drone had eerily buzzed overhead as I left an interview with an Afghan official.

As the day unfolds, I sense that aerostats and drones are the future of law enforcement in America, a future being ushered in by the rising clamor from those demanding that the US-Mexico border be sealed before immigration reform can be approved. Though not yet widely seen elsewhere in the United States, the usefulness of these devices is obvious for border surveillance and battling urban crime. These high-tech tools allow the constant monitoring of remote regions for illegal migrant crossings and round-the-clock surveillance of high-crime areas where law agencies can track criminal movements before and after crimes.

Aerostats are godsends for police departments that must do more with less. Aerostats mean concentrating a limited number of patrolmen in high-crime areas, helping them make arrests more quickly, taking the bad guys off the street, and making communities safer.

Yet these aerostats—surveillance balloons and the cameras they carry—can trample personal privacy. People expect to be shielded from the roving eyes of airborne video and infrared cameras. Although most people assume that the right to privacy is protected by the US Constitution, it is not. It is inferred. Privacy rights advocates point to the Fourth Amendment of the Constitution, which affirms the right "to be secure in their persons, houses, papers, and effects, against unreasonable searches and seizures." Privacy advocates also argue that just because the right to privacy is not specified, the Ninth Amendment supports privacy since it states that when certain rights are not listed in the Bill of Rights, it does not mean people don't have them. In addition, the Fourteenth Amendment protects citizens against "unreasonable search" actions by state and local authorities.

Privacy is very much on the mind of Alan S. Frazier, an assistant professor at the John D. Odegard School of Aerospace Sciences at the University of North Dakota and a specialist in mini-drones. These devices look like model airplanes but can cost up to $175,000 each and use battery power to stay aloft for as long as ninety minutes. They can be folded up and easily stashed in the trunk of a police car. If police are chasing a suspect, they simply launch one of these camera-mounted mini-drones using a slingshot-like catapult, and on a laptop display screen can track a suspect down alleys, across backyards, and to wherever he or she might try to hide.

"We need to be very sensitive to [privacy]," Frazier tells the expo, to prevent confrontations with hostile residents. "Don't keep it covert," he advises. "The public should know about this. Make sure you involve your community" before mini-drones are deployed. Frazier suggests a local advisory council to oversee aerial surveillance programs such as the one at the University of North Dakota, a panel of about fifteen people whose job is to certify that operations are ethical. To garner public support for mini-drones, Frazier suggests that "we need to be using this for humanitarian operations." Once the public becomes accustomed to these mini-drones, he says, the move to covert operations is easier.

Since the drones are virtually silent, Frazier says, and "sound like a mosquito," they quietly hover over locations about to be raided by police. Most fly about two hundred feet above the ground, but some can fly up to six hundred feet, which makes them even more difficult to detect with the naked eye. Frazier ticks off the applications: crimes in progress, tracking criminals from crime scenes, traffic control, covert surveillance, finding lost people, and marijuana eradication. The tall stands of North Dakota corn can hide marijuana fields in the middle of cornfields. The best way to find the marijuana is a mini-drone fly-over, he says.

The mini-drones are working their way into the national law enforcement arsenal, Frazier says, and have been employed in Colorado, Florida, and Washington State. Only about three hundred of the nation's seventeen thousand police departments have these devices. One of the vexing aspects of mini-drones, Frazier complains, is that private citizens don't need certification or a license to fly them, but government agencies do. Toy airplane aficionados balk at such licenses, yet the Federal Aviation Authority is devising rules that govern mini-drones flown by law authorities. When the police mini-drones eventually take to the skies, it may be too late, Frazier says. "The bad guys have the technology now. I guarantee that the crooks have it."

## Tracking Juárez Killers

Aerial surveillance has exposed ugly realities of law enforcement in Juárez, says Ross McNutt, president of Persistent Surveillance Systems. His company's surveillance cameras are mounted to the bellies of single-engine aircraft that fly patterns at high altitudes, allowing the cameras to record in high definition everything that happens in a sixteen-square-mile area. "We can watch a whole city at once," he says. But to do so is not cheap. The service costs $2,000 per hour, according to the company's website.

The system works much like Google Earth, McNutt explains, allowing the user to move around an urban or rural area using a laptop and a mouse, and zoom down to street level for close-ups at any time. The system can be rewound so a criminal can be traced back to his or her point of origin and followed after the crime. "We can watch a necklace being stolen off the neck of a grandmother," McNutt says, and know where the perpetrator came from and fled to after the crime. The system has infrared capability and is equally effective at night.

Employed by the city of Compton, the notorious crime-riddled community of Los Angeles, California, McNutt describes how his cameras observed a drug-dealing house that was visited by 130 vehicles in a four-hour period. This told officers where the dealer resided and the movements of the buyers and sellers, if not additional stash houses for drugs.

Hired by Juárez, Mexico, McNutt's company recorded thirty-four street murders, one of which he plays for the expo: a female Mexican police officer being shot by an apparent cartel gunman. McNutt tracks the movements of the killer and his accomplices before and after the event on computer-generated maps.

The police officer's murder was a contract killing, McNutt says, since the assassins seemingly knew the target's home and habits. Prior to the assassination, the killers drove to a nearby location, parked their vehicles, and fanned out, covering possible routes of escape. The designated hit man shot the woman at point-blank range on the street. The killers and witnesses were tracked as they fled, some returning to gang headquarters or retreating inside their homes or stores.

The Juárez police were not called until ten minutes after the killing, which allowed the killer time to get away, McNutt says. The precise moment the killing took place was recorded and compared to police records as to when the crime call came into the police station. The aerial video was provided to the Juárez and Mexican federal police along with the vehicle identifications and the location of the suspect gang headquarters, complete with street-level views. Yet the Mexican authorities dropped the case, says McNutt.

The case illustrates the pervasive corruption of the police and government, a topic that has been extensively documented in books by writers like Charles Bowden, author of *Murder City* and *Down by the River*, both chilling looks at the realities of the drug wars in Juárez. Also among his work is *El Sicario* (The Assassin), edited by Molly Molloy and Bowden, which is the autobiography of a high-ranking officer with the Mexican police who also worked as a hired killer for a drug cartel. The former assassin explains how one-third or more of any class at the Mexican police academy was on the cartel payrolls, earning much more per month from the cartels than the government. The cartel killers were being trained in programs funded and supported by US anticrime and drug-fighting agencies. Since the cartels have penetrated the Mexican military and law enforcement, little is done by either without the other knowing about it. Elements of the Mexican police effectively have been an arm of the drug cartels, far from independent enforcement arms of the Mexican government.

The cartels' corruption of law enforcement, if not the political system itself, points to the desperate need for a thorough reevaluation of the approach taken by the United States in the so-called drug wars, especially in regards to any cooperative programs with the Mexican government. How can the United States continue to throw money at a problem with the assumption that it will be spent properly and produce the expected result? It is wrong to assume that foreign actors have the same or similar interests as do Americans or will approach a problem and a possible solution the way Americans would.

## Over Land and Sea

With use of aerial surveillance looming in American skies, its application for monitoring the US-Mexico border is obvious. The aerostats of Logos Technologies LLC of Fairfax, Virginia, which have hung over the skies of Afghanistan, says David Luber, have been deployed along the US-Mexico border. During an eighty-hour test period, one such aerostat led to some 126 migrants being apprehended after they had crossed the border illegally, he says. The balloons help direct border agents through rugged terrain where the migrants hide. "We can tell an agent to turn left and go another fifteen feet" should migrants be hiding in dense brush, Luber says. "We're also able to backtrack in time," revealing crossing points and the positions of the spotters who monitor border agent movements. Such surveillance helped discover migrants at Nogales' commercial port of entry who were hidden among stacks of pallets in a large fenced enclosure.

But aerostats are effective for only short periods, Luber cautions. Since they can be seen from both sides of the border, the number of people attempting to cross in an area under surveillance quickly drops to zero as crossing routes are moved to unobserved areas. "Those folks know what they're doing," Luber says of the migrant smugglers.

Although aerostats have been found to be useful along the border, drones are considered the most effective way to monitor vast expanses of oceans, where about a third of all cocaine from South America is brought to US shores via semisubmersible submarines made of wood and fiberglass. Only a top hatch breaks the waterline, making them virtually invisible to the naked eye or radar. Propelled by diesel engines and with a range of nearly three thousand nautical miles, they can travel nonstop from the South American shoreline to the California coast.

For submarine surveillance, Paul Nelepovitz, an assistant professor of unmanned aerial surveillance systems at Embry-Riddle Aeronautical University, of Prescott, Arizona, likes the Predator B, the full-sized drone made by General Atomics of California. With a thirty-six-foot-long body and a wingspan of sixty-six feet, the Predators fly up to twenty-four hours and easily track the semisubmersibles, he says. High-resolution cameras carried by these drones can read the names on oceangoing vessels from an altitude of sixteen thousand feet.

They're not as widely used as one might think, at least not yet, Nelepovitz says. Only about ten were employed in the United States at the time, out of an authorized Predator aerial armada of about twenty-four. The Predator drones are parked at Fort Huachuca, Arizona, for work along the US-Mexico border; Grand Forks, North Dakota, for surveillance along the US-Canadian border; Corpus Christi, Texas, for surveillance along the Gulf Coast; and Cape Canaveral, Florida, for observation along the East Coast.

Months after the expo, an indicator of the future of drones in America will surface in early March 2013, when US attorney general Eric Holder sends a widely reported letter to Republican senator Rand Paul of Kentucky. Paul had conducted a filibuster against the confirmation vote on President Obama's nomination of John Brennan to head the CIA. The filibuster ended when Holder clarified the administration's views on the use of military force, including the use of drones, inside the United States. Holder explained that, yes, the president does have the authority to use military force against American citizens on US soil—but only in "an extraordinary circumstance." If the executive branch of government can use drones against threats inside the United States, use of drones to control crime seems tame by comparison. Paul responded by calling the policy "an affront to the constitutional due process rights of all Americans."

## Perceptions and Realities

I exit the conference exhausted, leaving the filtered air and fluorescent lights for the warmth and sun of the late El Paso afternoon. I sit on a low wall and close my eyes. With drones and aerial surveillance systems tracking Mexicans scurrying across the border, life as it once was along the border is gone forever.

I make my way to the University of Texas at El Paso, a bustling institution where Spanish is the language most often spoken by the students I pass on the street and in the hallways. And why not? The students here are largely of Mexican descent, attending college in their quest to claim a piece of the American dream, just like European immigrants of earlier epochs. The university is a crucible of cultures, epitomizing borderland realities.

I find Josiah Heyman, professor of Anthropology and chair of the Sociology and Anthropology Departments at the university, in one of its older buildings on a low hill in the campus. He welcomes me into his spacious office and settles behind a desk piled high with papers. His answers to my questions come quickly, since I'm one of many journalists who have come here from around the world hoping to unravel the riddles of the US-Mexico border.

Perceptions are perhaps more powerful than reality, Heyman suggests. The image of Mexico that has been cultivated over decades, if not centuries, is of the "source of all things bad," Heyman says. That image has been reinforced recently by the gruesome carnage of the drug wars.

The United States' relationship with Mexico is largely economic and transcends border issues and culture. "This is a commercial economy," Heyman says. "It is a North American thing." US trade with Mexico exceeds $1 billion per day, totaling nearly $400 billion a year, and is more than all US exports to Brazil, Russia, India, and China combined. Trade with Mexico also supports manufacturing and jobs in the United States, since more than 60 percent of the products the US imports from Mexico contain US-made parts. Trade with Mexico creates US jobs, Heyman says.

While US business with Mexico booms, the cartel drug wars in Juárez and elsewhere in Mexico dominate news from south of the border. That should not come as a surprise, Heyman says, because the United States is the largest drug market in the world. Someone else would supply that demand if the Mexicans didn't. The 2006 data from the Office of National Drug Control Policy in the White House states that Americans spend at least $100 billion per year on illegal drugs: $38 billion on cocaine, $11 billion on heroin, $18 billion on methamphetamine, and $34 billion on marijuana. Consequently, the fight for dominance over the exporting *plazas* such as Juárez is understandable. But, Heyman says, Mexico also has a drug-use problem, which contributes to the drug problems along the border. "It is also about Mexican demand."

The economics of the illegal trade with Mexico is not one-way, Heyman says. The assault rifles and pistols that are the tools of cartel enforcers and foot soldiers are trafficked from the United States into Mexico. "It's also true bad things come out of the US and into Mexico."

The reality along the border cannot be reduced to good guys in the United States versus the bad guys across the border. "It's a double-sided process, and it flows back and forth," Heyman argues. "It is not confined by a neat border. It's really a big system."

Exacerbating the situation is the endemic corruption of Mexican politics. "Mexico has a legacy of corruption," he says; it is the grease that lubricates a feeble government nominally in control of what amounts to a narco-state.

The decades-long rise in drug use in America, the growth of the drug cartels, and the United States' longstanding war on drugs have created mutual dependencies, Heyman says. Agencies such as the Drug Enforcement Administration and the newly reconfigured, reequipped, and expanded border agencies depend on a high level of illegal activity along the border—the smuggling of both people and drugs—to justify their existence. The "quasimilitary bureaucracies and the cartels . . . need each other," Heyman says, in a dynamic of "mutual reinforcement."

Regressive drug policies in the United States have been "encouraging the growth of illegal drug" trafficking, he says. The demand for illegal narcotics has created an enormous black market in the United States, and the cartels have responded by establishing networks of distributors and enforcers here. "It is clear continental drug organizations operate extensively in the US." The business has become so profitable that the Mexican cartels have evolved into "transnational drug organizations."

Heyman criticizes America's war on drugs with good reason. Over the past forty years, ever since President Richard Nixon formed the Drug Enforcement Administration in 1973 and proclaimed "an all-out global war on the drug menace," the US government has spent an estimated $2.5 trillion fighting illegal drugs. Despite crackdowns on smuggling, a rising number of arrests, and mandatory jail terms for drug dealers and users, the number of chronic drug users in America has increased to more than twenty million Americans, or about 6 percent of the population, according to government statistics from 2006. Occasional users bump the number of drug users to more than thirty million, or about 10 percent of the population.

But after four decades, drugs arrive more easily than ever. "US enforcement has not significantly decreased the flow of drugs," Heyman says. An indicator is the price. "The general trend for the price of drugs in the US has gone down in the past thirty years," he says, because of the law of supply and demand. As the demand for illicit narcotics has grown, so has the supply, which has dropped the price dramatically over the past decades. This was borne out in a July 3, 2012, article in the *New York Times* citing data from the DEA that the street value of a gram of pure cocaine in today's market is $177.26. Adjusted for inflation, a gram of cocaine is 74 percent cheaper today than it was thirty years ago.

The falling price for a gram of cocaine makes any argument for continuation of the war on drugs verge on ridiculous. It offers no rational justification for the expenditure of billions of dollars annually to wage a war that has been an abject failure and has led to the loss of tens of thousands of lives in Mexico. The drug war further burdens the US economy with the cost of incarcerating the tens of thousands of people on drug and drug-related offenses, many of which may have been minor and largely victimless crimes.

A better approach, Heyman suggests, would be to attack America's $100-billion-per-year drug habit. "The use of drugs is generally damaging to human health," Heyman says, and the public health threat posed by drugs is often cited by antidrug enforcement agencies as justification for their work. But that same public health argument has not been equally applied to the same well-documented and damaging effects of tobacco and alcohol, Heyman notes. The public health argument has not been used to call for the expenditure of billions of dollars to wage a war on tobacco and alcohol. Instead, these two widely used and addictive products are legally and readily available. Yet, Heyman says, it is well established that just like cocaine, heroin, and methamphetamine, "tobacco has enormous negative health effects."

Attacking America's drug habit can be effective, Heyman says, just as the demand for tobacco products has declined dramatically "due to a comprehensive national awareness campaign." Consumption of tobacco has dropped from 50 percent of the population to 20 percent and is a "huge accomplishment in the war on drugs [because] people have been educated. The culture has been manipulated."

Likewise, Heyman says, "There are other ways of approaching drugs," but these have been largely ignored. Marijuana, for example, "has a low level of harm" compared to tobacco and has proven to be "nonaddictive," despite a reputation of creating a psychological dependency. This suggests that public policy should focus less on marijuana compared to harder drugs such as cocaine, heroin, and methamphetamines, he says, freeing law enforcement resources to focus on other crimes.

Decriminalizing marijuana could also have far-reaching effects on cartel violence. Marijuana provides an estimated 40 to 60 percent of annual cartel income, Heyman says. If marijuana were grown legally in the United States, "we could cut [cartel] income in half. That we are not [doing that] is scandalous."

Steps in that direction have been taken with the legalization of marijuana in Washington and Colorado in the November 2012 general election. In 1996 California became the first state to allow medical marijuana. Connecticut, Massachusetts, and Oregon are expected to legalize marijuana in the coming years.

Although the legalization of marijuana challenges federal law that bans it, how this will play out in the courts remains to be seen. For the short term, President Obama has indicated that the federal government will not resist Colorado and Washington's legalization.

People are prone to "self-medicate," Heyman says, and have done so for the duration of human experience. But how much is too much? Since many Americans feel the need to consume drugs and alcohol in copious amounts, another way to control and discourage the use of drugs would be better counseling and mental health services. Provide people with the skills they need to deal with life's travails, he says, without reflexively reaching for a bottle of alcohol, a vial of pills, a joint, or a gram of opiates at the first sign of trouble.

"I don't want to let Mexico off the hook," Heyman says, noting that the roots of the cartels and their violence are political and social. For most of the twentieth century, Mexico was controlled by one party, the Institutional Revolutionary Party (PRI). A semi-authoritarian regime that was considered corrupt by most standards, the PRI was able to keep control of drugs and organized crime, he says. This well-entrenched order was lost at the turn of the century, however, when the National Action Party rose to power in 2000, replacing the PRI.

Although this change was seen by many as the flowering of democracy in Mexico, it also meant that the traditional power structure was lost. "It became unbound," Heyman says. "Controls over criminality were reduced." This came at a time when the large crime groups fractured and went to war with one another. "Now there's a lot of rivalry between criminal organizations." These changes were set against the backdrop of a weak and corrupt judiciary, since Mexico "never had much of a criminal justice situation," Heyman says. Consequently, drug and crime organizations grew in size and strength.

For most of the twentieth century, the Mexican Army was used to control criminals and dissidents, Heyman notes, and admittedly was "corrupt and quite nasty," even down to the low levels. In the newly elected Mexican regime, the role of the army was in flux and no longer an enforcement tool for only the entrenched political elite.

"The war on drug organizations has amplified the size of the Mexican Army," Heyman says, which in 2006 was brought to bear by former president Felipe Calderón against the growing strength of the cartels. There is a "gray zone between the police and the army," Heyman says. The strongest of the law enforcement bodies is the Federal Judicial Police, which has "no sense of human rights and due process," he says, but adds, "It's not a uniquely Mexican problem."

The United States has not been sitting on the sidelines while the Mexican government has struggled with cartel violence. In 2008 the United States launched the Merida Initiative, a multiyear, $1.6 billion project to funnel equipment and expertise to Mexico to strengthen judicial and law enforcement agencies. Helicopters and fixed-wing aircraft were sent to bolster counternarcotics operations. Prosecutors, defenders, investigators, and forensic experts were trained in Mexican and US law schools. Alternative justice centers provided mediation for minor offenses. Police were trained and a corrections academy for Mexican federal and state correctional staff was set up. Scanners, X-ray machines, and other inspection devices, along with trained dogs, were given to Mexican authorities for use at major checkpoints and ports of entry. Money was sent to help protect journalists and human rights defenders.

The war on drugs should be waged as aggressively inside the United States as it is waged outside, Heyman says, if America expects to make any progress against the strong headwinds of the drug trade. "We need a long-term drug-use reduction policy," he says. "We need to downsize the criminal organizations [and] their capacity to commit crimes." This can be done best by reducing the flow of money to cartels by reforming policies on drugs such as marijuana. America's war on drugs needs to change because "drug interdiction has been a miserable failure. We are breeding more sophisticated criminal organizations."

The cartels now control illegal immigration and human smuggling. "People used to cross the border without the criminal organizations," he says, but no more. This lucrative cartel business could be eradicated by reforms to US immigration policy that allow work visas for migrants. Such an expanded visa program would permit "getting people legally to jobs and will save thousands of lives."

Though Heyman's arguments make sense, I return to the expo to discover that the tactics used to address the problems in America's borderlands are going in quite another direction.

# 4

# MIGRANTS OR TERRORISTS?

❈

**With the war in Iraq now history** and the war in Afghanistan winding down, there is money to be made in securing the US-Mexico border. When the doors are flung open to the exhibition hall of the Border Management Conference and Technology Expo, this becomes clear: I encounter a camouflaged and heavily armored vehicle looking like the ubiquitous Humvees of Iraq and Afghanistan. It is just the kind of vehicle one would want for traversing the rugged terrain of southern Arizona. Neither the thick tires nor the steel armor nor the camouflage paint job are important. It's the sensing device atop the telescoping mast that rises through the roof hatch with a high-resolution camera and infrared thermal sensor that attracts attention here. The telescoping masts can be fitted onto the beds of heavy-duty pickup trucks, and six weeks later I will discover what these camera and sensing devices can do as I accompany Border Patrol agents on a night patrol.

The telescoping mast and camera are part of an array of products on display at the expo. Aerostats float above the exhibition hall, and laptop screens reveal what the expo looks like from the eye of the hovering camera. There are paintball guns that shoot pepper-spray rounds, which I will later shoot; hand-held communications systems; and ground-sensing devices. Tables are covered with specialized glossy magazines with titles such as *Border & CBRNE* (chemical, biological, radiological, nuclear, and explosive) *Defense, Tactical ISR Technology* (intelligence, surveillance, reconnaissance), and *The Counter Terrorist,* lending this confab its distinctly militaristic air.

A ground-sensing system is promoted by Glenn Spencer, an Arizona resident and California transplant who is one of the nation's most notorious critics of what he believes are the government's inadequate efforts to secure the border. Called Identiseis, the system uses a string of ground sensors connected to seismographs and a computer to detect people and animals walking nearby. Spencer and his business associates at Border Technology Inc. demonstrate the system, which has been placed on his property along the US-Mexico border, via a real-time video screen.

While many companies at the expo are start-ups, some are behemoths of the defense contracting world: Lockheed Martin, Northrop Grumman, Panasonic, and Philips. The expo sponsor is General Dynamics, a $32-billion-a-year defense contractor with a workforce of about ninety-five thousand people, according to its website, that builds combat vehicles, runs shipyards, provides secure information technology systems, and makes Gulfstream private jets. The conference was organized by the Institute for Defense and Government Advancement, which offers security-themed conferences around the world and matches contractors with government buyers, illustrating the global reach of America's military-industrial machinery.

Any doubts about the militarization of the US-Mexico border are dispelled when Felix Chavez, deputy chief of operations with the US Border Patrol, tells the expo that the agency's mission is "to protect America . . . to prevent the entry of terrorists and terrorist weapons" into the country. In the minds of the masters of border security, the threats posed by jihadi terrorists are blended and blurred with the Mexicans who desperately cross the border in search of jobs.

Rather than capturing terrorists, as Chavez suggests, the Border Patrol has been doing a good job at collecting migrants who cross the border illegally. In 2000 a total of 1.64 million migrants were apprehended. Ten years later, with the doubling of the size of the Border

Patrol to about twenty thousand agents, the number of apprehended undocumented migrants dropped 80 percent to just 327,000 in 2011, according to the Customs & Border Protection statistics. The cause of this precipitous drop is a matter of heated debate. These statistics comprise the quiver of sharp-tipped arrows used by the advocates of more and better border enforcement. But statistics alone do not reflect reality, argue immigration reformers, who insist that the decline is largely the result of fewer jobs in America because of the depressed economy. Mexican migrants will find a way to cross the border no matter how much enforcement is at the border, they argue, as long a good jobs are available.

If statistics do anything, they present a big-picture view of activity along the border. Of the total apprehensions in 2011, about one-third, or 129,118 people, were picked up in Arizona, followed by Texas with nearly another third at 118,911, California with 72,638, and New Mexico with 6,910. A total of 396,906 people were deported in 2011, which includes about 50,000 people who were already in the United States illegally. Nearly five million pounds of narcotics were confiscated in 2011, a 20 percent increase over fiscal year 2010, and $126 million in undeclared currency was seized. The number rose slightly in the federal fiscal year that ended in September 2012, when 357,000 people were apprehended. Apprehensions will continue to rise in the federal year ending September 2013, when more than 420,000 immigrants are captured, a 15 percent increase over the previous year. More than half of the apprehensions are along the Texas-Mexico border, indicating that the majority of illegal crossings have shifted from Arizona, which previously led the nation, to the less secured areas along the reaches of Rio Grande. Although these numbers suggest that the Border Patrol is doing its job well, little mention is made of the fact that preventing a terrorist threat is the reason for the exponential growth in border security. No known international terrorists were among those apprehended at the border.

Like all government agencies, the Border Patrol anticipates budget cuts as the national dialogue bears down on runaway congressional spending and the mushrooming national debt. "We're taking the capabilities we've got," Chavez says, and directing them against the terrorist threat and the drug cartel smuggling routes. Drones are the key.

Less than a month later, a five-year, sole-source Border Patrol contract with the country's leading drone maker, General Atomics Aeronautical Systems of San Diego, California, will be reported in November 2012 by the Center for Investigative Reporting. Said to be worth about $443 million, with about half of that money going to buy fourteen new drones, the deal doubles the agency's fleet of ten drones. The drones will not only fly the two thousand miles of the US-Mexico border but also patrol the four-thousand-mile-long Canadian border and patrol both coasts. The CIR reports that the agency wants the Predator B, costing $18.5 million each, and the Guardian, which costs about $20.5 million and is to fly over coastal waters. The drones will "allow us to manage" the border, Chavez tells the expo. "The intent is to disrupt the smuggling cycle" and to "stop illegal activity" along the border.

In fact, the agency's budget is not a problem. Nearly twenty-five years ago, in 1990, the Border Patrol survived on a paltry $262 million. By 2011 the budget ballooned to $3.5 billion, a thirteenfold increase. At nearly $500 million, the proposed drone program has been lambasted for being nearly 15 percent of the agency's budget.

## Jihad North and South

The presumed terrorist threat is not poised along America's Southwest border. Quite the opposite, says Professor Bert Tussing, director of homeland defense and security issues at the US Army's War College and an authority on border security. Canada is the "conduit of choice for terrorist activities." It is a stunning admission, given that border security has been overwhelmingly focused toward Mexico. In fact only about thirty-two of the entire four thousand miles of the US border with Canada can be called secure, Tussing says.

Tussing points to the infamous Millennium Bomber of December 1999—a terrorist named Ahmed Ressam, who wanted to blow up the Los Angeles airport. Ressam was stopped with one hundred pounds of explosives in the trunk of his car at Port Angeles, a town atop the Olympic Peninsula of Washington State, after having crossed to the United States on a ferry from Victoria, British Columbia.

Ressam was originally from Algeria but moved to France in 1992 and on to Canada in 1994. Detained by Canadian authorities for having a crudely faked passport, he was allowed to stay after he applied for political asylum. He lived in Montreal for the next four years, surviving, by his own admission, on welfare and theft.

Ressam came in contact with members of an Algerian terrorist group called the Armed Islamic Group, linked to al-Qaeda. When Ressam's application for asylum was denied in 1995, he dropped from sight and assumed a new identity by forging documents that resulted in a Canadian passport with the name of Benni Noris, which he used to try to enter the United States. Ressam had traveled to Afghanistan in 1998, where he joined a terrorist training camp funded by Osama bin Laden and hatched his bomb plot.

On the afternoon of December 14, 1999, Ressam made his move, driving a rental car onto the ferry at Victoria, crossing the Strait of Juan de Fuca, and landing at Port Angeles. Ressam had passed a preliminary check at the Victoria port since a scan of his Canadian passport did not reveal convictions or arrest warrants. At Port Angeles, however, an agent became puzzled at his answers to routine questions. When a thorough search of the car revealed the explosives, Ressam ran. He was caught.

After a four-week trial in US District Court in Los Angeles in April 2001, Ressam was convicted of conspiracy to commit an international terrorist act, explosives smuggling, and lying to customs officials. Facing life in prison, Ressam testified against his coconspirators and provided information about his terrorist network. Then, just days after the 9/11 attacks, Ressam was interrogated in prison near Seattle, and said he knew none of nineteen hijackers. But he provided details of "sleeper cells" in North America.

Terrorist trouble could be percolating in other remote regions, Tussing explains. Hezbollah, the Lebanese terrorist organization, reportedly has cells in the triborder region of South America, where Argentina, Brazil, and Paraguay meet. The threat posed by such a group is unclear despite statements on some conservative blog sites. In early 2013 the Breitbart News blog claimed that Hezbollah "is now expanding to the north, teaming up with dangerous Mexican drug cartels and engaging in weapon trafficking in and out of Mexico." The site noted that the US House Committee on Homeland Security has explored the issue and proclaimed that "Hezbollah is also teaching the drug cartels how to build elaborate tunnels under the US-Mexico border. The tunnels are almost identical to the ones the terrorists built under the Gaza-Egypt border. Cartels are able to smuggle drugs, humans, and weapons into the US with these tunnels." Tunnel technology, however, may be a poor indicator of links between cartels and terrorist groups, let alone a mounting threat. Cartels could be exporting their skills, not the other way around.

Others have weighed in on the issue, however. An October 2011 report titled *The Mounting Hezbollah Threat in Latin America*, by the conservative think tank the American Enterprise Institute for Public Policy Research, claims that Hezbollah has a growing presence in the West. Written by former assistant secretary of state for Western Hemisphere Affairs Roger Noriega and *Foreign Policy*'s Jose R. Cardena, the report states, "Over the last several years Hezbollah and its patrons in Iran have greatly expanded their operations in Latin America. . . . Today, Hezbollah is using the Western Hemisphere as a staging ground, fundraising center, and operational base to wage asymmetric warfare against the United States. Venezuela's [late] Hugo Chávez and other anti-American governments in the region have facilitated this expansion by rolling out the welcome mats for Hezbollah and Iran." Though the Hezbollah threat may be a plausible concern, there is little or no concrete evidence that "rolling out the welcome mats" is anything more than a show of anti-American solidarity.

A more immediate threat, however, is that the Mexican drug cartels have established ties with violent gangs in Central American countries, such as MS 13 of Guatemala, where gangs "outgun local law enforcement," the same report states.

Security threats beyond US borders "cannot be expected to remain over there," Tussing warns, as the attacks of 9/11 showed, but he takes a moderate position when it comes to on-the-ground practicalities of border security. Dealing with an unformed terrorist threat is important but also requires a "new mind-set," he says, because the United States cannot, for its own economic welfare, seal the Mexican border. A balance must be found between security and the economy, Tussing suggests. "Most of the people crossing the border are doing so for economic opportunities" and provide an endless supply of cheap labor. "We have to remain open to that as much as we can." Turning off the flow of people and goods across the border is not the answer.

## Not Quiet on the Mexican Front

The threat posed by global jihadists is far from the front lines of border protection where people like John Smietana Jr., chief agent for the Big Bend Sector of the Border Patrol, fight a lonely battle against overwhelming odds on a remote section of the Rio Grande. His district is where the Rio Grande swings from south to north, then bends southward for a long run to the Gulf of Mexico. In most countries a river presents an obstacle, but not here. "The river is almost nonexistent most of the year. You can drive across it," Smietana says.

The Big Bend area is rugged and remote, with sculpted rock buttes, high canyon walls, and scorching desert, yet it is a battleground in the cross-border drug wars. The Mexican town of Ojinaga has been a *plaza* and a cartel enclave. While the sector captured about four thousand undocumented migrants in 2011, it also grabbed fifty thousand pounds of marijuana, undoubtedly a fraction of what is being brought across. Better surveillance and intelligence has helped, Smietana says. "We can pretty much tell what the bad guys are doing," but that does not make their work less dangerous. Local ranchers have been threatened, their border fences cut, and weapons stolen from their homes, he says.

Now the Mexican government wants to reopen a rail line across the border, and Smietana is not happy. "It's a concern to us to have the rail line open again. Smuggling is a business, and when we stop one thing, they're going to find another." One of those "others" is the use of ultralight aircraft, he says, but "we don't shoot them down." The only time drug smuggling seems to stop is when the cartels are fighting one another, he says.

Rodolfo Karisch is chief of the Del Rio sector, south of Big Bend and also on the Rio Grande. His region has more action than Big Bend, in part addressed by his horse patrol unit. The sector had an all-time high of 157,000 arrests of undocumented migrants in 2000, and that number dropped to 19,000 arrests in 2011. With that came the seizure of nearly 90,000 pounds of marijuana in 2010, the confiscation of 441 rifles—more than half of which are military-style assault weapons, 200,000 rounds of ammunition, and 32 hand grenades.

In the Del Rio sector, the land flattens and the Rio Grande becomes wide and shallow, with thick brush growing along both sides where it flows into Lake Amistad. Karisch says he needs a device that penetrates the dense foliage along the river, excellent cover for drug and human smuggling. Karisch also wants an aerostat to help his agents monitor vast sections of the river and Lake Amistad without having always to be physically present. "What they use in Afghanistan will work in Del Rio. If we have the technology . . . we may not need so many agents."

Karisch oversees some sixteen hundred agents, yet feels overwhelmed even with a fleet of twenty patrol boats for the lake. "The bad guys just try to wait you out and then cross," he says. Often the smugglers are better equipped than the Border Patrol. The region is remote and communication can be spotty. Agents have chased gun-toting smugglers using satellite phones, Karisch says. Agents have also nabbed smugglers wearing uniforms of legitimate oil companies and driving tankers loaded with drugs, illustrating the sophisticated techniques cartels use to move their products through ports of entry and into the United States.

Karisch attributes a drop in contraband seizures to the killing of some top cartel capos by the Mexican government. "That disrupts their operations," at least for a while, he says. "That is why we are seeing a downturn in contraband."

Smuggling stops can quickly turn violent, Karisch warns, and over the past few years, nine agents have been attacked. But smugglers prefer not to get violent with US citizens or officers, since it's bad for business, he says. His agents prefer not to be overly aggressive, he says, because "if you look for violence, it's going to find you."

Leslie Lawson is the patrol agent in charge of the Tucson Sector/ Nogales Station, which is among the busiest of all border ports of entry. With the hardening of urban borders to the east and west, the Tucson sector has become the focus of the immigration influx. The sector station has about seven hundred agents patrolling one thousand square miles and thirty miles of border. It's barely enough, Lawson says. "A lot still needs to be done due to the volume of people coming across."

For the federal fiscal year ending in September 2012, the sector nabbed twenty thousand people, an increase of 10 percent over the year before, and confiscated 122,000 pounds of marijuana, 149 pounds of cocaine, and 951 ounces of heroin. Agents were assaulted more than seventy times, she says. Lawson has units on bicycles, all-terrain vehicles, and horses, with drug-sniffing dogs at the ports of entry and at interior checkpoints.

The sector uses telescoping devices, cameras, and ground sensors, but the rugged terrain makes it hard to transmit signals from sensors back to the command center, Lawson says. "The mineral content of the soil messes with communications." Improved roads in the back-country have helped. "It's been a game changer for us," she says.

The border at Nogales has drainage tunnels between Mexico and the US that are used by smugglers. During the rainy season, "It can be very dangerous," Lawson says, even though the drains are dry most of the year. "People are smuggled through those, [as well as] drugs."

As the agency throttled the drains, cartels turned to tunnels. In 2001 agents uncovered twelve tunnels, and more have been found each year, with six uncovered in 2012. "They dig by hand, use jackhammers and unemployed miners," Lawson says. Some tunnel discoveries have been so fresh that agents smelled cigarette smoke and heard voices of people scurrying back to the Mexican side.

In late December 2012, just a few months after the conference, yet another tunnel is discovered in Nogales by Mexican authorities, based on a tip. It is more than one hundred meters long and equipped with electric lights and ventilation. The Border Patrol says the tunnel, which was apparently still being built, does not extend into the United States.

Marijuana is the drug most frequently confiscated, Lawson says, because it is least expensive and therefore easiest to lose. "We don't find people backpacking hard narcotics," since "they're going to be much more careful with those" because of the costs.

Even so, the drug and human smugglers are increasingly hard to spot in open country. "We are finding aliens are using camo and desert camo to blend in," Lawson says. She hopes to get better field sensors so that when her agents respond to an alert, they will know if they're about to confront cows, migrants, or armed drug smugglers. Agents "need to know what they're going to encounter."

The militarized border is supposed to confront a perceived terrorist threat, drug smugglers, and the flood of undocumented migrants. Is it the right approach? For answers, I return to the University of Texas, El Paso campus.

# 5

# OVERWHELMING ODDS

⚜

**The modern Mexican drug trade** dates from the 1920s and 1930s, explains Howard Campbell, professor of anthropology at the University of Texas at El Paso and a leading authority on the drug wars and cross-border culture. Campbell is the author of *Drug War Zone: Frontline Dispatches from the Streets of El Paso and Juárez*, a book that details the past and present of the drug trade from the inside out, revealing the perspective of the men and women who have been the street dealers and small-time smugglers.

The Mexican drug trade originated in states such as Sinaloa, a practically autonomous region that has produced marijuana and opium poppies brought from China. One of America's earliest anti-drug laws came in 1875 when San Francisco banned the opium that had been brought by the Chinese laborers imported to construct the transcontinental railroad. As with all drug laws, prohibition did not diminish demand, but it may have pushed poppy cultivation from California to Sinaloa, where it could be grown relatively freely and then smuggled north into the United States, effectively germinating Mexico's multibillion-dollar narcotics business.

Over the decades, it became a tradition "to bring drugs to the US and to Mexico City," from these provinces, Campbell says. Notorious narcotics dealers were often backed by politicians and included people such as La Nacha, a woman known for supplying drugs to Beat Generation personalities of the 1950s such as Neal Cassady and writers Jack Kerouac and William Burroughs. Sinaloa produced "black tar heroin," popular because it's cheaper than white heroin, though less potent. Likewise, marijuana was brought into the United States by the stream of migrants who crossed the historically open border seeking work and trade.

Drug dealing mushroomed with the hippie culture of the 1960s, Campbell says, an era when smoking marijuana was almost mandatory, prompting comedians such as Robin Williams reportedly to quip that if you remember the 1960s, you weren't there. "The 1960s moved marijuana into the mainstream," Campbell says. The 1970s witnessed the rise of cocaine, and after serving primarily as a pipeline for South American cocaine, Mexico's drug dealers eventually controlled the business. "In the early 1980s, the Tijuana Cartel is big and outrageously violent" and controls Tijuana, Campbell says. In Juárez another major cartel developed headed by Amado Carrillo Fuentes, known as the Lord of the Skies because of his fleet of cargo planes that brought cocaine from South America to Mexico.

Campbell has been a resident of El Paso since 1991, and his book grew out of a class he taught at UTEP. One of his students, Jose Trinidad Carrillo, worked at the Immigration and Naturalization Service until the day Carrillo was arrested in connection with twenty-one tons of cocaine seized in a Los Angeles warehouse. Campbell realized how deeply embedded the drug trade was in the Juárez–El Paso community and the culture. "It is something that everyone knows about but doesn't talk about," he says. "I call it the Juárez–El Paso cartel. The business is here. Once those drugs come through Juárez, they're [in El Paso] at least for a little while. The [drug trade] is deep" and drug running is a "multigenerational" tradition.

Campbell waves toward his office window and the city beyond, telling me where I can find a neighborhood of used car lots and body repair shops in which vehicles are modified and panels welded to hide drugs that are carried across the Rio Grande from Juárez to El Paso.

El Paso is filled with "huge warehouses and stash houses" where drugs are held for shipment to locations throughout the United States.

The drug trade is part and parcel of the daily life along the length of the US-Mexico border, as Campbell explains in *Drug War Zone*:

> There is a virtually limitless supply of unemployed workers ready and willing to make good money by driving or walking loads of drugs across the border or by serving as a stash-house guard or a hit man. Smugglers have little difficulty adapting socially or communicating in Spanish, English, or Spanglish on either side of the bilingual, bicultural border. The enormous maquiladora industry and related El Paso long-haul trucking industry provide the heavy-duty eighteen-wheelers and every possible storage facility, tool, equipment, or supply needed to package, conceal, store, and transport contraband drugs. The binational conurbation also provides all necessary banking, currency exchange, telecommunications, legal, and other services required for an effective drug-smuggling organization. Likewise, black-market guns and stolen cars used for self-defense and smuggling are readily available. Thousands of local residents live simultaneously in both El Paso and Juárez, and families bisect the border. In essence, the border is more a resource for smugglers than a hindrance.

The realities of life in the borderlands have evolved over time, Campbell says, but only when the violence reached a horrific level was any attention paid to it. "Multiple wars broke out [over the *plazas* and smuggling corridors], and the worst was in Juárez."

"Why such extreme violence?" I ask.

"In some ways, it's a fad," he says. It started with a video of an execution in 2005 that was posted online, and this evolved into a "competitive show of gruesome destruction."

Tougher US immigration policies have exacerbated border conditions, Campbell says, contributing to the evolution of a criminal counterculture. "The US has made it worse by making immigration harder. Now [there] is a population of frustrated youth" in Mexico who are unemployed, uneducated, and can't get into the United States. They turn to the cartels for work and money, and become "cannon fodder" for the drug wars—those who end up dead on the streets of Juárez. They're called the "*ninis*," Campbell says, a shortened version of "*ni estudia, ni trabaja*," meaning they neither study nor work. "The result of the [US] policy was to create this situation." Campbell compares the situation below the border to the Middle East, where unemployed youth have turned to fundamentalist Islam to find meaning for their lives.

A critical step toward lowering cartel violence, Campbell suggests, would be to ease visa restrictions so that more migrants can work legally in the United States. This would take a lot of otherwise unemployed Mexicans off the street and allow them to find gainful employment far from the clutches of the cartels. Staunching the flow of automatic weapons and assault rifles from the United States into Mexico is a second vital component to lowering the death toll. Finally, shrinking America's demand for narcotics is necessary, although Campbell is doubtful that will happen. "The US drug market won't lessen," he predicts, and smuggling is unlikely to slow.

## An Exercise in Futility

My sense of the futility of the war on drugs grows exponentially the next day at the expo, when independent filmmaker and author Gary "Rusty" Fleming reveals the murky and bloody world of the cartels. Fleming's book, *Drug Wars: Narco Warfare in the 21st Century*, published in 2008, resulted from his three years of travel in the borderlands, where he investigated the workings of the Mexican drug cartels, an experience riddled with horrifying revelations. Fleming was "embedded" with a branch of the Gulf Cartel, which controls much of the eastern coast of Mexico along the Gulf of Mexico and has been at war with the Zeta cartel over that territory.

"They run a multibillion-dollar business," Fleming says of the cartels. "The worse they look, the better it is for them," which explains the cartel's use of horrific violence as a way to frighten away both competition and law enforcement. The cartel killers will do "anything that puts out the message 'Don't mess with us.' They will kill twenty people to get to the one they want." The Zetas, who began as an elite group of special forces intended to combat the cartels, were trained by the US military in Fort Benning, Georgia, Fleming says.

Although the gruesome killings by the Zetas and other cartels have been confined to Mexico, the cartels' reach extends deep into US cities, the ultimate market for their drugs. "They've established very sophisticated networks in the country," Fleming says, working through local gangs in at least twenty-five of America's largest cities. It is a very calculated business approach, and the enforcement of the system is brutal. "These are not a bunch of coked-up cowboys," he says. "Whatever they need, they can get."

The cartels have been aided greatly by the North American Free Trade Agreement, which went into effect on January 1, 1994, and established the world's largest free trade zone, linking more than 450 million people in Mexico, the United States, and Canada and generating an annual trade of several trillion dollars in goods and services. While NAFTA has been a boost for the economies of all three countries, it also opened the door to the drug cartels. About 80 percent of all of the narcotics that enter the States come through the legitimate ports of entry, Fleming says. "The narcotics are camouflaged by all that commerce." Some eight thousand vehicles cross into the United States each day from Mexico, he says, and of that number, only a small fraction are thoroughly inspected. "The odds are pretty good that you're going to get your product across." The profit motive is high, Fleming says, because the estimated wholesale value of illegal drugs crossing the border is about $40 billion a year, and that translates into a street value three times that, or about $120 billion annually.

Street gangs in the United States control the retail drug market in most American cities, Fleming says, which has propelled homicide rates in inner cities such as Chicago and Detroit, something that has been reiterated by top law enforcement in both cities. The gang violence is due to "merger, acquisitions, and hostile takeovers," Fleming says, which follows the simple rule known as "silver or lead." Deals are sealed with either money or bullets, and "lead is cheaper than silver," he notes.

Drug cartels control the Mexican government, Fleming says, and with the tens of thousands dead on the streets of Mexico over the past years, it is clear that "the government cannot protect its people." The cartels dictate who lives and who dies in Mexico. "Once they seize the territory, they run everything," he says.

Fleming offers a simple explanation for the very low death rate in El Paso compared to Juárez, which is just across the river. "The narcos all live here," he says of El Paso. "They're not going to fight a war here. You don't want to kill the goose that laid the golden egg."

Fleming concurs with Campbell that El Paso is a critical "transshipment" point for drugs entering the United States. The drug cartels own trucking companies, he says, and have used trucks to haul car motors to Detroit along with thousands of pounds of drugs.

The cartels are increasingly sophisticated in their recruiting in Mexico, Fleming says. They no longer want street thugs, so-called cash dummies who sell small amounts of drugs on the street for cash. They're expendable and easily replaced. "They want clean-cut, educated, smart kids," Fleming says, ones who can use computers and have good business sense. "These are not a bunch of idiots and thugs," he says of cartel captains. "They love young and good-looking girls [to work with them] because they're less suspicious." Fleming claims that the cartels offer college tuition to prospective members and encourage them to obtain university degrees. The cartels are planning for the long term, he says, and are placing their recruits in law enforcement, the legal system, and throughout the banks and economic matrix.

Young cartel members between the ages of seventeen and twenty-four are also being recruited in the United States, especially in borderlands, Fleming says. The Zeta cartel calls them the "Zetillas," or little Zetas. Fleming had contact with one young man said to have killed at least forty-five people in the past half-dozen years, a grisly trade he began as a young teenager. The price for each hit rose from $5,000 per kill to $50,000 in just a few years. He became admired and feared by his peers, spending lavishly and driving an expensive European car.

## Not Over, Not Lost

Although the drug-war battles along the border seem bleak, the war is not over, nor is it being lost, counters Joseph Arabit, special agent in charge of the El Paso Division of the Drug Enforcement Administration. Millions of people and vehicles cross the border each year, and the maquiladoras exist among a proliferation of warehouses that Arabit admits are "used as covers" for drug shipments. The job of law officers in El Paso is to keep the violence in Mexico from spilling into the United States, he says, while curtailing the flow of drugs.

El Paso is quiet compared to Juárez, not because the cartel leaders may live there, Arabit says, but because of "a very large, very collaborative law enforcement organization on this side." It includes city, county, and state police, and federal agencies such as the DEA, the FBI, ICE, and Homeland Security. When something happens, they collectively attack the problem, Arabit says. Coordinated law enforcement has also helped Juárez drastically reduce the number of murders on the streets of the city. Reaching a peak in 2010 with more than 3,100 killings, the number of Juárez homicides dropped below 2,000 in 2011 and to just 680 in 2012.

"We identify the assassins in Juárez," Arabit says. "We link them to a crime in the US. Once we get them indicted, the Mexicans will go and pick them up. It's progress. Law enforcement in the US has played a part. We are having a positive significant impact in the US and Mexico." Some of the arrests made in the past year or so have been of "people who run multiple hit squads" and who have conducted multiple daily killings. "We've had some impact there." With the US and Mexican authorities working together to solve the problem, Arabit hopes that the crime rate in Juárez will eventually revert to what it was a decade ago.

According to the Mexican police, Arabit says, 70 to 80 percent of the killings were done by and were of street-level dealers, so the Mexican police began to attack the problem on that level. "They went out and arrested hundreds of people. They focused on the street dealers. They declared marshal law."

How the United States has worked with Mexican authorities to cut crime in Juárez is illustrated by how both entities handled the March 13, 2010, shooting death in Juárez of a pregnant US consulate worker and her husband. Juárez gunmen left the couple's traumatized baby crying in the backseat of the car as they fled the scene. That same afternoon in Juárez, gunmen also killed the husband of another US consulate employee and wounded their two young children, who were also in the vehicle. The shootings took place in broad daylight as the victims headed home from a party at a colleague's home in Juárez, according to news reports.

The shootings were the first such attacks by cartel gunmen on US government employees and their families, who were so seemingly removed from any direct involvement in the drug wars. The killings drew an outcry from the White House and prompted the State Department to let consulate employees move their families across the border into the El Paso area for their safety.

But it didn't end there. Some nine months later and after an extensive investigation on the US and Mexican sides of the border, Mexican police began arresting members of Los Aztecas, a cross-border gang in Juárez and El Paso, said to be hired guns of the Juárez Cartel and responsible for much of the violence in Juárez. After his arrest, the apparent leader of Los Aztecas, Arturo Gallegos Castrellon, a.k.a. "Benny" Gallegos, claimed to have ordered about 80 percent of the killings in Juárez during a fifteen-month period from August 2009 extending well into 2010, including that of the US consular employees. If true, he was responsible for the deaths of some two thousand people.

Gallegos also admitted to ordering an earlier attack in Juárez on a gathering of teenagers that left fifteen partygoers dead, sparking outrage on both sides of the border. Gallegos said that the killers believed rival gang members would be at the party.

Though the killing of the three US consulate workers captured US attention, an interrogation of other arrestees revealed that the consulate workers may have been targeted because they had issued visas to members of a rival gang. An alternate explanation was that the killings were ordered because the consulate workers had leaked information about the Los Aztecas and their companion gang in El Paso known as the Barrio Azteca. Like Los Aztecas, they were allied with the Juárez drug cartel, which at the time was fighting the rival cartels for control of Juárez.

On June 29, 2012, more than two years after the consulate killings, the US Justice Department announced that Gallegos had been extradited to the United States to stand trial for his role in the March 2010 shootings. He was among a total of thirty-five gang members on both sides of the border who were charged with crimes including racketeering, narcotics distribution and importation, retaliation against persons providing information to US law enforcement, extortion, money laundering, obstruction of justice, and murder. Of the thirty-five defendants, ten were Mexican nationals, including Gallegos. Of the thirty-five charged, thirty-three were apprehended, twenty-four pleaded guilty and were serving extended sentences, and one committed suicide while in prison. Six others were awaiting extradition from Mexico.

Violence often follows the money, Arabit says. "Every investigation we do here, we have a financial component" that looks into the flow of funds across the border. "The money laundering side of any cartel is very compartmentalized," so that even inside the cartels, the left hand does not know what the right hand is doing. The DEA depends on a system of informants, he says. "We try to keep those informants very activated."

The law agencies also rely heavily on "fusion centers," intelligence gathering and analyzing offices that are part of a wide-ranging domestic surveillance system that incorporates private contractors, the federal government, military, and local law enforcement databases. The centers were organized by the Department of Homeland Security and the Department of Justice to provide federal authorities with access to local databases and other information concerning law-breaking and law-abiding citizens. More than seventy fusion centers are scattered across the country, one of which is in El Paso, and most are at undisclosed locations that use post office boxes as addresses.

The reach of the DEA is deep into Mexico, Arabit says. The agency has eleven offices in Mexico and has been operating there for thirty years. The battle against drugs and cross-border crime is constantly evolving, he says, and demands higher levels of technology to keep abreast of the cartels. "The traffickers are changing [tactics] on a daily basis," he says.

While legalization of such drugs as marijuana might lessen the enforcement burden on the DEA, Arabit opposes it. "We're not in favor of legalization," he says, because the drug problem cannot be solved with just one simple solution. Legalization does not address the detrimental health effects of widespread drug use that legalization permits.

"We lose sight of the cost to society," Arabit says. "Study after study says marijuana is a gateway drug." Enforcement of drug laws sends a message throughout society that drug use is bad, Arabit says. "People have to feel the pain of it," he says. "For arrests that warrant jail time, they're going to jail," he says of offenders. "We are doing the best we can to tell kids that drugs ruin lives."

Arabit's position reflects the longstanding argument of antidrug enforcement agents, but the national trend is clearly in the opposite direction. And for good reason, as Professor Heyman has explained. After billions of dollars have been spent on the war on drugs, the result has been to bestow brutal drug cartels in Mexico and elsewhere with inconceivable wealth and power. That wealth and power derives from the kind of antiquated drug laws Arabit has sworn to uphold. Clearly the situation calls for another approach, one that includes legalization and regulation of drugs like marijuana and a sweeping public education program that can, as the antitobacco campaign has shown, dramatically reduce the demand. Not only would it improve the health of Americans, but it would also save billions of dollars that can be used elsewhere, while undermining the revenue that has turned drug cartels into multinational criminal organizations.

## Mexico's Drug Problem

While America's demand for drugs is insatiable, Mexico struggles with its own growing addiction problem. In the border town of Agua Prieta, Sonora, some months after I was in El Paso, I find the Center for Rehabilitation and Recuperation of the Illness of Drugs and Alcohol, a drug addiction treatment facility, as the name implies. The center deals with a largely unreported aspect of the Mexican drug trade—Mexico's own serious drug addiction problem.

Some estimates from 2009 suggest that at least 3.5 million Mexicans have used narcotics at least once and that about 600,000 are regular users. This compares to approximately 22 million regular drug users in the United States. Yet a more critical indicator is that the number of addicts in Mexico appears to have doubled from 2004 to 2009. As I soon learn, many in Mexico attribute the increase in drug use to better US border enforcement, which has forced Mexican drug cartels to create a drug market in their own country. Infighting among the cartels may have also contributed to the problem, as fractured groups of dealers strike out on their own, selling to whomever they can.

Many at the Agua Prieta treatment center were drawn into the drug trade at a very young age by the cartels, says director Raoul Garcia, and most have sold drugs in the United States. "Because of the US's militarization of the border, the cartels are selling more here. It's harder to get it into the US." The center is treating about sixty men and ten women at the time of my visit, including women ranging in age from their teens to their eighties, Garcia says. The center is sparse, with a minimum of comforts, and the walls of the meeting hall are painted with the dictates of the twelve-step process and the Serenity Prayer.

Garcia introduces me to Benny, who lived many years in Washington State and in Tucson. He has relatives across the border in Douglas, Arizona. The drug problem is much worse in Agua Prieta than most people think, Benny says, explaining that drug dealers are on most street corners. He agrees that stricter border enforcement has made it harder to get drugs across, so to compensate for the drop in business, the cartels are pushing drugs in Mexico. "[Cartels] wanted to get me to drive it across," he says, but he refused. Now the cartels are recruiting young people in the United States to help them and are trying to bribe Border Patrol agents, he says. "In twenty years, the cartels will have people working for them" in key positions in the government and private industry on both sides of the border.

Benny's family settled in Agua Prieta, he says, after his father and uncle were deported. His grandmother sold her house in Tucson and bought land in Agua Prieta, where the family now resides. Benny likes the center because it allows him to come and go. "Here you have more leverage. They give you a chance to work and bring food in." A crack addict, he admitted himself to the center because he "wanted to get high again." Benny became involved with drugs when he was eighteen, when he was asked to sell some. "I was trying to help someone else out. It had to do with the [lack of] money I had in my own pocket at the time."

"Have you kicked your addiction?" I ask.

Benny shakes his head no. "I'll probably go back to my addiction. I came here to kick back."

Another addict, Cristobal, has used heroin, crack cocaine, marijuana, and peyote, he says, but has been clean for twelve years. "The only way the addicts can help each other is this way," he says, motioning to the twelve-step process painted on the wall. "There is a higher power, and because of that, I am free of drugs. I learned to say no to drugs."

The symbiotic nature of culture and crime in the borderlands has affected and linked many people, families, and lives. One community that is a prime example of this connection is the historic border town of Columbus, New Mexico, where a dozen people, some of them public officials, their families, and their friends, were drawn into the dark periphery of the drug cartels. It has not gone well for them or the town.

I am also drawn to Columbus because just about one hundred years ago, the town was the focus of national attention when Mexican revolutionary Pancho Villa and his army rode across the US border in 1916 and attacked the town. The US response was swift, and an ill-fated force was sent deep into Mexico to find Villa. It failed in that mission yet set what became an ironic precedent for US-Mexico relations.

# III

★ ★ ★

# GUNS, MONEY, AND RESENTMENT

# 6

# GUNS GO SOUTH

✳

**In the predawn hours of March 10, 2011,** helicopters pounded the night air over Columbus, New Mexico. On the ground, heavily armed federal agents fanned throughout the town, bursting through doors and arresting ten residents. The suspects included the town's police chief, the mayor, a town trustee, and some family and friends. An eleventh suspect could not be found and a twelfth was charged later.

All but the fugitive were ultimately convicted for their roles in a gun-smuggling operation that put nearly two hundred high-powered weapons into the hands of apparent Mexican cartel killers. The weapons included the highly prized AK-47-type pistols and 9mm handguns, along with military-style body armor. The AK-47 pistols are similar to the well-known Kalashnikov semiautomatic rifles but have shorter barrels and a pistol grip instead of a shoulder stock, which makes them easier to carry and use at close range. They are also prized because they use the same caliber of bullets and high-capacity magazines as the larger versions.

The Columbus culprits included Eddie Espinoza, the fifty-one-year-old mayor; Angelo Vega, forty, the Columbus police chief; Blas "Woody" Gutierrez, thirty, a town trustee; Ian Garland, fifty, of Chaparral New Mexico, the gun dealer who sold most of the weapons; Gabriela Gutierrez, the wife of Blas Gutierrez, who was later charged in the smuggling operation; Eva Gutierrez, twenty-one, the sister of Blas Gutierrez; and Ricardo Gutierrez, twenty-five, a cousin of Blas Gutierrez. Others charged were Miguel Carrillo, thirty, of Columbus; Alberto Rivera, also of Columbus; Manuel "Coruco" Ortega, twenty-five, of Palomas, Mexico; Vicente "Tito" Carreon, of Columbus; and Ignacio "Nacho" Villalobos, twenty-four, also of Columbus, who escaped arrest and remains a fugitive.

For the fourteen months between January 2010 and March 2011, according to the federal indictment, the Columbus ring bought weapons from Garland's Chaparral Guns, a business that he based out of his house in Chaparral, New Mexico, a semirural area just north of El Paso. The group then sold the weapons and tactical body armor to buyers across the border thought to be members of a drug cartel. Although the exact circumstances were not revealed, investigators said that twelve of the weapons the group had purchased were later found at crime scenes in Mexico and were retrieved by Mexican authorities. The guns were then traced back to the defendants.

The Columbus gun-smuggling operation is a tale of greed, audacity, and abuse of civic power. It is also a cautionary tale of the corrupting power of the cartels that spills over the Mexican border and deeply affects the social and cultural ties that bind communities along the border together. Ironically, the Columbus case drew none of the national attention of the Fast and Furious operation conducted in neighboring Arizona by the federal Bureau of Alcohol, Tobacco, Firearms and Explosives (ATF). Yet the Columbus case resulted in convictions for almost all involved, unlike Fast and Furious.

The investigation began in mid-January 2010 when Blas Gutierrez and Miguel Carrillo obtained three AK-47 pistols, two Ruger .45 pistols, and three FN 5.7 pistols, most of which were purchased in Arizona. The Rugers were among the weapons later recovered in Mexico. Although it is not specified in the indictment, investigators in New Mexico and the El Paso region may have been tipped off to the activities of the two Columbus men since Arizona was then the focus of the controversial Fast and Furious operation that tracked the sale of nearly two thousand high-powered weapons from Arizona gun shops into Mexico, the same weapons used to kill victims in the cartel drug wars.

The undoing of the Columbus smugglers was the violation of a seemingly innocuous provision of federal gun laws contained in what is known as Form 4473. Required by the ATF, the form must be filled out and signed by the buyer of a weapon affirming that he or she is the ultimate owner of the weapon, and that it is not being purchased for resale. Violating the terms of Form 4473 is a federal offense.

With the help of at least one undercover informant, federal investigators began tracking gun purchases made by Blas Gutierrez and others in what became a wide circle of family and friends, all customers of Chaparral Guns. The gun buying went slowly at first, with months passing between purchases, but picked up in July 2010 with two purchases that month, followed by two more in August, seven in September, and six in October. Most of the purchases in September and October were made by Blas Gutierrez and Alberto Rivera, and were of up to ten weapons in a single day.

Former mayor Espinoza was brought into the ring in the fall of 2010, and on October 4 Espinoza signed papers to buy five tactical 9mm pistols and one AK-47-style pistol, according to the federal indictment. Espinoza and Chief Vega may have been nervous about their scheme, because just four days after Espinoza's gun purchase, he and Vega stopped several federal agents who were driving around Columbus and asked them what they were doing in town. Although the presence of federal agents might have raised suspicions among Gutierrez, Vega, Rivera, and the others, the group seemingly ignored it and other encounters with law officers, apparently assuming their positions in town government shielded them from suspicion. They were wrong.

Rather than lying low, just days after the encounter, Espinoza leased an apartment in a middle-class neighborhood in the heart of El Paso for $1,200 per month, intending to use it as a stash house. Then in November 2010 Espinoza claimed that his friend, Blas Gutierrez, was actually his son and listed him as an occupant of the apartment, hoping that their comings and goings would not arouse suspicion. The leasing of the apartment set the stage for the gun smuggling to shift into high gear.

In early January 2011 Blas Gutierrez drove an unmarked pickup registered to the Columbus Police Department to make a gun purchase at Chaparral Guns, according to court records. Eight days later, on January 13, he returned to Chaparral with Ricardo Gutierrez and Alberto Rivera, and among the three of them, they purchased a total of thirty-one weapons that included AK-47-type pistols and 9mm pistols. Four of the weapons bought that day were recovered just two months later in Mexico.

By January 2011 the gun business was going well for the Columbus ring, according to the indictment. Eight AK-47 pistols were purchased from Chaparral Guns on January 20, another five AK-47 pistols were purchased on January 24, followed by twenty more 9mm pistols on January 25. With the twenty pistols in hand, Blas and Ricardo Gutierrez, along with Ortega and Carreon, drove to the El Paso apartment, where they loaded the guns into a black backpack. Ortega and Blas Gutierrez, who continued to drive the police department's pickup, then went to the El Paso bus station, where they apparently put the backpack loaded with weapons on a public bus or handed them to a contact who took them to Juárez.

Two days later, on January 27, Ortega and Carreon returned to the apartment, where they met with a woman, presumably a contact with the Mexican cartel. According to the indictment, the woman drove a Honda Pilot with Mexican license plates and had crossed the border into the United States just an hour earlier. The men took a large black suitcase out of the Honda and into the apartment. Two hours later they hauled the suitcase out of the apartment, and again using the city's pickup truck, took the suitcase to the bus station, where it was handed off.

February got even busier, and as the gun purchases became bigger, federal agents began to close in. Unaware that they were under surveillance, members of the ring asked Garland to order an additional forty weapons while continuing to buy smaller lots of weapons, five and ten at a time.

The indictment indicates that Nacho Villalobos, who remains a fugitive, may have been a liaison between the cartel gun buyers in Mexico and the Columbus ring. Most of the purchases were made following orders by Villalobos for weapons, sometimes with very specific details, including body armor. On February 10, 2011, for example, Blas Gutierrez and Chief Vega purchased what is described as "thousands of dollars' worth" of combat gear and body army "at the direction of" Villalobos, as well as another ten AK-47 pistols, which were signed for that evening by Ricardo Gutierrez and picked up the next day, February 11, by Blas Gutierrez.

Also on that day, the indictment states, gun shop owner Garland told Gutierrez that the forty additional AK-47 pistols they had ordered would be delivered that evening, prompting Gutierrez to promise that two others from the group would sign for that bulk purchase. The day following, Mayor Espinoza and Miguel Carrillo signed for some of those guns, which were loaded into several duffel bags and taken to the apartment stash house for safekeeping.

Unknown to the group, however, their gun-smuggling operation was about to unravel.

That evening Blas Gutierrez and his sister, Eva, again went to the Chaparral gun shop, where Eva signed for ten AK-47 pistols. Instead of taking the weapons to their stash house, however, they drove back to Columbus on New Mexico Highway 9, a lonely two-lane road that closely parallels the US-Mexico border. Suddenly, the flashing lights of a squad car came up behind them. The two were pulled over by what is described in the indictment as "law enforcement," and the weapons were confiscated.

This should have instilled panic in the group, in particular Blas Gutierrez, since it was obvious that authorities knew that he was traveling with ten freshly purchased weapons and that investigators knew about their dealings. Instead, the indictment states, Gutierrez told Eva to get another $4,000 in cash to buy ten more AK-47 pistols to replace the ones that had just been confiscated. Apparently, Gutierrez was worried that he and others would suffer consequences if the weapons were not delivered as promised to their suspected cartel buyers.

That evening, Blas Gutierrez called Espinoza and told him what had happened to their guns. Rather than recoiling at the news, Espinoza agreed to call the authorities to demand the weapons be returned. The following day, February 13, Vega also agreed to make some calls, asking Blas Gutierrez for the name of the officer who had taken the weapons.

As this was going on, federal agents quietly raided the ring's stash house and took twenty of the AK-47 weapons, along with thirty high-capacity magazines and a grinding tool used to remove the serial numbers from weapons so they couldn't be traced.

On February 14, just two days after Blas and Eva Gutierrez were stopped on the highway, Blas Gutierrez and Chief Vega discovered that the twenty weapons were missing from the stash house. According to the indictment, the two discussed the missing weapons and speculated that maybe their partner Coruco Ortega had already shipped the pistols across the border to their Mexican buyers. Not quite sure, however, Gutierrez made a call to Mexico to their customers and explained that they had "problems" with the planned weapons delivery. Blas then called Nacho Villalobos and discussed what they were going to tell "the people in Mexico" about the missing weapons. Blas Gutierrez and Chief Vega then decided to buy a gun safe to protect their next batch of gun purchases, oblivious to the fact that investigators were circling them.

The next day, Garland got a call that the group was sending someone to his shop to pick up the remaining twenty AK-47 pistols, the final half of their forty-weapon purchase. On February 16 Vega made good on his promise to try to recover the confiscated weapons and, according to the indictments, promised a federal agent that Blas Gutierrez was doing nothing illegal with the vast number of weapons he'd been buying.

The gunrunning operation took yet another strange turn, according to the indictment, when Blas Gutierrez and Chief Vega drove to Albuquerque, where they picked up a shipment of "bulk cash" and returned to Columbus, a round trip of at least eight hours. The money, the amount of which was not disclosed, was then smuggled into Mexico, suggesting that this trip may have been a separate task for the men assigned by their cartel contacts, unrelated to the gun smuggling.

About a week later, Blas Gutierrez and Alberto Rivera made yet another trip to Garland's Chaparral Guns shop and bought another ten AK-47 pistols, then headed back to Columbus rather than their El Paso stash house. Gutierrez again was stopped by authorities, and the weapons, along with more than fifteen hundred rounds of ammunition, were confiscated. Despite having been stopped twice by police, who confiscated their recently purchased guns, the group remained unfazed. Instead of fleeing the state, if not the country, or attempting to cover their tracks, they did nothing as the federal noose was tightening on their gun operation. According to the indictment, on the same day the second batch of weapons was confiscated, Vega placed another call to a federal agent in hopes of securing the return of the weapons, again insisting that Gutierrez was not sending the guns to Mexico.

Two weeks later, the group was arrested, charged, and imprisoned. Over the following year, most of the defendants pled guilty to various charges and were convicted. On March 15, 2012, more than a year after the initial arrests, Vicente "Tito" Carreon became the first of the group to be sentenced for his role in the operation, and was sent to federal prison for three years and ten months, to be followed by three years of probation.

On May 25, 2012, gun dealer Ian Garland was sentenced to five years in a federal prison followed by three years of probation for his role in the selling of the 193 weapons, most of which were smuggled into Mexico. At the sentencing, Garland reportedly told the judge, "I did what I did. I am responsible for my actions. I just worry a lot for my family. We're losing the house."

The federal judge, Judge Robert C. Brack, had little sympathy for Garland, according to an Associated Press story on the sentencing. "There is a war in Mexico and the war machine requires fuel," Brack told Garland. "This conspiracy was happy to supply that fuel. What made my decision was that in this terrible supply chain, that link was you."

Less than a month later, on June 14, 2012, Espinoza was sentenced to four years and three months for his role in the smuggling. Then on October 9, 2012, another four in the case were sentenced after having entered guilty pleas. Rivera was sent to prison for twelve years; Ortega, a resident of Palomas, received five years and ten months; Carrillo received forty-six months in jail; and Gabriela Gutierrez, the wife of Blas Gutierrez, received two years in prison. Each was given an additional three years of probation. As of this writing, Vega and Blas, Ricardo, and Eva Gutierrez have been convicted and are awaiting sentencing.

The Columbus gun-smuggling ring illustrates the corruptibility of border communities and the cross-border reach of the cartels. But it also lays bare the gaping holes in US gun laws and exposes America's role in enabling, abetting, and profiting from the horrific killing being carried out by cartel gunmen in towns and cities along the border and throughout Mexico. More than once these killings have spilled into the United States.

## Not So Fast and Furious

On the night of December 14, 2010, Border Patrol agent Brian Terry tracked a group of Mexican armed bandits, *bajadores*, who prey on vulnerable Mexicans who have just crossed the border, robbing them, raping them, and stealing whatever drugs they may be packing. Terry was part of the elite Border Patrol tactical group BORTAC and was in rugged terrain about ten miles north of Nogales, Arizona, just west of US Interstate 19 in Peck Canyon. The *bajadores* opened fire on Terry and three other agents. Despite Terry's combat experience as a US

Marine for three years with a tour of duty in Iraq, one of the bandits got behind him and shot him in the back, according to Border Patrol reports. Terry died aboard a rescue helicopter en route to the hospital. Two weapons were collected from the scene.

Terry's tragic death highlighted the dangers in the borderlands and lifted the lid on one of the most controversial gunrunning sting operations ever conducted by US law enforcement authorities. Initially known as Project Gunrunner, a George W. Bush–era program to staunch the flow of weapons into Mexico, the project took a bizarre turn in the Phoenix office of the ATF. Because the initial program was criticized for not producing results, it was renamed Fast and Furious and recast as an operation to let weapons cross the border in hopes of capturing the cartel bosses doing the buying. It didn't work.

In late 2009, according to national news reports, ATF officials were alerted to a growing number of suspicious gun buys being made in seven Phoenix-area gun shops. Buyers were paying cash, often brought in brown paper bags, and the weapons of choice were those favored by the cartels, AK-47 pistols. Even at that early date, gun shop owners alerted the bureau's agents, who reportedly told them not to worry; the ATF was going after the big fish, not the small-fry buyers.

Among the buyers was Jaime Avila, a young man who had been watched as early as January 2010 and who was eventually charged, convicted, and sentenced to prison in the Terry case. Over the next year, the ATF watched as Avila and others bought as many as 575 of the AK-47 pistols, claiming all were for personal use. According to news reports, nearly 2,000 weapons were bought under the noses of ATF agents, including powerful 50-caliber Barrett sniper rifles, which require a bipod to support the barrel.

Despite the decision to let the guns "walk" across the border, nearly a dozen agents protested the policy, some predicting that a US agent would eventually be killed by one of these weapons. A CBS News story on the Fast and Furious scandal quoted an unnamed agent as asking a superior, "Are you prepared to go to the funeral of a federal officer killed with one of these guns?"

That officer unfortunately was Terry. The serial numbers of the assault weapons recovered at the scene of Terry's shooting were traced and showed that Avila had purchased the gun presumed to have been used to kill Terry from the Lone Wolf Trading Company of Glendale, Arizona. Within hours of Terry's death, Avila was apprehended, leading to the arrest of nineteen others who were also indicted.

One of the key whistleblowers in the case, which prompted congressional hearings, reports, and congressional sanctioning of US Attorney General Eric Holder for his lack of cooperation, was federal senior agent John Dobson. Assigned to the Phoenix office of ATF in 2010, Dobson told news reporters and congressional investigators that his job was to stop guns from going across the border, not help them. Despite the claims by the Justice Department that the ATF never knowingly allowed the sale of weapons to suspected gunrunners, the argument seems incredulous since national television networks broadcast surveillance video that showed suspected cartel buyers carrying boxes of AK-47 assault rifles to their cars parked at a Phoenix-area gun shop.

ATF agents were well aware of the connection between the gun deaths in Mexico and escalating gun sales by the Phoenix-area weapons dealers. According to news reports, an e-mail from an ATF supervisor, later identified as David Voth, who supervised the Fast and Furious operation, noted that some 958 people had been killed in Mexico, about one-third of whom died in Juárez alone, during March 2010, one of the country's deadliest months ever. That month was also when the suspected gun buyers purchased 359 weapons just from the Phoenix area, Voth noted.

A detailed investigation into Fast and Furious was conducted by the Center for Public Integrity (CPI), a nonprofit, nonpartisan investigative news agency. Titled *ATF Let Hundreds of U.S. Weapons Fall into Hands of Suspected Mexican Gunrunners*, the CPI report probed the tortured tactics behind the operation. According to the report, in October 2009 the operation was run by a special team called Group VII, which was granted permission to let the federally licensed gun shops under their purview allow suspected cartel buyers to take weapons across the border. The center contacted Mark Chait, the ATF assistant supervisor for field operations, who explained that the bureau had come under fire for the lack of results in Project Gunrunner. Chait said that continuing to arrest the "straw" buyers of the weapons was not helping the agency capture any of the drug cartel capos.

According to the ATF, 1,765 firearms were sold during the fifteen months of Fast and Furious, and an additional 233 had been sold prior to the official sanctioning of the operation, for a total sale of 1,998 weapons. Not all of the weapons got across the border, the center reported. Of the total weapons sold, 797 were recovered at crime scenes in both Mexico and the United States. The remaining weapons have not been recovered.

The most vocal congressional critic of the operation was US Senator Chuck Grassley, an Iowa Republican, who spearheaded a congressional probe. The bureau seemingly did nothing with the information it had collected about the flow of weapons, Grassley complained. "The ATF clearly had plenty of information on the bad guys," Grassley told CPI. "The problem wasn't the fact that the guns weren't being reported, it was that the ATF didn't act on the information they had."

The Mexican government was incensed over Fast and Furious. Even the ATF attaché in Mexico City at the time criticized it, saying that the gun-walking operation sent the wrong message to the Mexican government. Gun possession is tightly controlled in Mexico, which led former president Felipe Calderón to say that it was clear that cartel weapons came from the United States, because of its lax gun laws. "[US] institutional cooperation [in the fight against cartels] ends up being notoriously insufficient," Calderon said, according to the CPI report.

In late 2011 it was revealed by news organizations and congressional investigators that some in the ATF operation were so disgusted with America's lax gun laws that they hoped the findings of the operation would prompt additional controls on gun sales. The additional control the ATF agents wanted was known as "demand letter three"—so named because it would be in addition to the two existing reports that licensed gun dealers must file with the federal government. Demand letter three would require gun sellers to report sales of not only individual weapons but also of multiple weapons sales on the same day to the same individual. The letter, if implemented, would affect most gun dealers in the four border states of California, Arizona, New Mexico, and Texas, where the drug cartels' straw buyers shopped. Gun rights advocates objected to demand letter three, claiming it violated Second Amendment rights.

Unlike the Columbus gun-smuggling case, Fast and Furious generated massive media and congressional attention. Yet the operation produced few arrests and only one conviction, despite the death of a Border Patrol agent. Many other straw buyers were apprehended in the operation shortly after Terry's death, but only Avila was convicted. He was sentenced to four years and eleven months in prison, according to news reports.

Prosecutors showed that Avila had spent about $60,000 to buy fifty-two weapons that included semiautomatic rifles and sniper rifles such as the 50-caliber Barrett. But Avila was not the only straw buyer, nor was he the most active, according to the federal indictment. Uriel Patino was the most prolific, having purchased more than three hundred guns, most of which were AK-47 assault rifles.

The nineteen other straw buyers tracked by Fast and Furious, almost all of whom were between the ages of eighteen and twenty-five, were released within twenty-four hours of their arrest and their charges ultimately dropped, according to a July 2012 report by Fox News. Most of the buyers were unaware of the consequences they faced for buying and selling the weapons and were just trying to make some extra money, authorities agreed, which amounted to about a hundred dollars per weapon bought, according to those close to the case.

Meanwhile, investigators would continue to work on the Terry case. In September 2013 US law authorities said the third of five suspects in the killing had been captured in Mexico and that work had begun to turn the man over to the United States for prosecution.

## Laws, Guns, and Money

In September 1994 President Bill Clinton signed into law the Violent Crime Control and Law Enforcement Act, which restricted the production, sale, transfer, and possession of military-style assault rifles. The law focused on a variety of weapons thought to be particularly dangerous because of their high-capacity magazines, which made them ideal for criminals and gang warfare. These weapons of war are designed to inflict the maximum physical harm with each and every bullet. This is not the effect sought by hunters, who hunt for sport and presumably prefer to eat their kill, rather than scrape animal flesh and fur from the surrounding tree bark.

The weapons banned under the law included the Automat Kalashnikov, or AK-47, and the Colt AR-15, now one of the fastest-selling weapons in the United States. In fact, an estimated three million assault weapons were sold after the law expired in September 2004. Several states have adopted their own assault weapons bans, however, most notably California, and those laws remain on the books.

The lifting of the federal assault weapons ban in 2004 had a dramatic impact on the drug cartel wars in Mexico. According to ATF data, compiled by the agency's National Tracing Center, the only gun-tracking facility in the United States, some 70 percent of the 99,691 weapons seized in Mexico between 2007 and 2011 came from the United States. The remaining 30 percent were from non-US manufacturers or had unknown countries of origin.

The numbers illustrate the deadly effect US gun sales have had on Mexico. The numbers cited by the tracking center represent only the weapons the Mexican government collected from drug cartel crime scenes and drug raids. Mexican authorities then asked the US government to trace the origins of these weapons. Many tens of thousands more are undoubtedly still circulating in Mexico and in the hands of cartel killers.

The weapons confiscated in Mexico pose another question: What is the percentage of the traced weapons compared to the total weapons actually in the hands of the cartels? Ten percent? Fifty percent? Twenty percent might be a reasonable guess, just for argument's sake, since criminals and cartels are not prone to giving up or leaving their weapons behind. If nearly 100,000 weapons were captured in Mexico over the five years from 2007 through 2011, that is an average of about 20,000 assault weapons and semiautomatic pistols captured each year. If those 20,000 captured weapons are only 20 percent of the annual total number of weapons regularly coming into Mexico, it suggests that about 100,000 such weapons could be flowing into Mexico each year. This means a total of about 500,000 weapons came into Mexico from 2007 through 2011.

According to ATF tracing data, 70 percent of those weapons came directly from the United States. Given my estimated annual total of about 100,000 weapons arriving in Mexico each year, that means about 70,000 were sold by US gun dealers each year from 2007 to 2011. That's 350,000 weapons over the five years. Enough for an army—a cartel army, which explains why the Mexican police and army have been fighting a losing battle against the cartels. Clearly, American gun sellers have enabled Mexico's drug cartels to kill some seventy thousand to ninety thousand Mexicans. While gun advocates might chafe at the accusation, noting that federal agents and not Phoenix-area gun sellers knowingly let weapons cross the border, the weapons sold during Fast and Furious were only a fraction of the total weapons that flowed south into Mexico.

According to Fast and Furious reports, the average price of an AK-47 pistol is about $650, and some other higher-priced pistols cost more than $1,000 each. Assuming a 20 percent profit for each sale, or about $130 for every AK-47 pistol and $220 for each higher-priced pistol, that adds up to about $12.2 million in profit each year from the sale of guns that end up in Mexico. According to a study titled *Cross-Border Spillover: U.S. Gun Laws and Violence in Mexico*, prepared by professors from the University of Massachusetts and New York University, most of those sales come from gun dealers in Arizona and Texas. Clearly, while Second Amendment rights are often recited as a cover for unbridled sales of weapons of all makes and models, the profit motive could be king.

The debate over gun control is agonizing, given that America's gun laws, driven by millions in profits by gun manufacturers and gun sellers, have contributed to the death of the estimated seventy to ninety thousand victims of the cartel drug wars in Mexico. But the effects of the gun laws have not been restricted to Mexico, as the arrests of the Columbus mayor, police chief, and others show. The aftereffects of the raid on Columbus still reverberate, as I soon learn.

# 7

# GOOD-BYE, COLUMBUS

✳

**The March 10, 2011, raid** on Columbus sent shock waves through the closely knit community, says Juanita Aguayo, who once worked at the Columbus Police Department with former chief Angelo Vega. "The first house they raided, it was getting toward dawn," she says, and was followed by other houses, including the police chief's. When Aguayo drove to the police station early that morning, "there was a bunch of vehicles and people trying to get into the office. In the end, it was kind of weird," she says.

Thinking back, a lot of things happened at the department that never made sense, Aguayo says, such as unknown people who were frequently stopping by the office and asking for Vega. "They were kind of scary." She cannot say precisely why, but Aguayo suspects that the environment at the police department put her on edge. "When you work at the police department, you're more alert." She had wondered about Vega long before the bust. "I thought he was undercover," she says, but never discussed it. "I could always go and question him. He was always good to me. Other people had a problem with him."

Her suspicions about the department began when she tried to bring order to the department's budget, having been a bookkeeper at her previous job. "Nobody paid attention to that stuff," she says. "I tried to make a spreadsheet of equipment purchases," she says. Instead of using it, "they took it away from me."

When Aguayo learned that the chief, the mayor, and others had been selling weapons into Mexico, she took it personally. "I was very upset. I have family in Palomas," the town just across the border. "I've always lived there." In 2008 and 2009, the years leading up to the gun-smuggling operation, Palomas was the site of cartel violence that included the kidnapping and killing of the town's mayor, an event that had been preceded by the mass resignation of the Palomas Police Department in the face of cartel death threats. In 2008, according to reports, the once quiet town of eighty-five hundred residents had forty homicides, making it statistically more deadly than Juárez.

Aguayo remembers those days well. "You felt it. You didn't want to go to Palomas. You saw a lot of people you'd never seen before. It was like a little Juárez." On weekend evenings, young people would cruise the town for entertainment, but when the violence escalated, "it stopped. Cars would follow you. It was scary. It was very tense. You were in survival mode." Because the small-town atmosphere was ruined, "it was becoming a ghost town" as several thousand people left. But the quiet has returned, she says, and the town is recovering. "There's a lot more people going out at night. You feel a little bit safer. People are getting a little bit more comfortable."

## Under Siege

Martha Skinner, Columbus's former mayor and seventy-six-year-old owner of Martha's Place, a cozy hotel and one of the town's few thriving businesses, remembers the raid well. "That was something else," she says with a note of disgust. "They snuck into town at 3 AM and by 5:30 AM we were up. I thought it was Afghanistan. I thought we were under siege." Agents used helicopters and flares. "We were getting reports that the mayor was in handcuffs." An acquaintance who works with Immigration and Customs Enforcement called her later that day, asking, "'How'd you like that?' We were all in shock. It took me a week to recover."

The chagrin that Skinner harbors from the raid extends to those who were ultimately convicted, all of whom she knew. "They were selling guns to Mexico so they could kill each other down there. It's beyond me. They had a good cover in [Police Chief] Vega," Skinner says; he was "an easy target" to enlist in the scheme. Blas Gutierrez "was the focus of the action" and brought his relatives into the ring. She describes him as "the sweetest young man," who changed as he grew older. "Most of them were in it for the money," she says, though she also suspects that drugs may have played a role. "If we never saw them again," she says of the group, "it would be fine with me. What [former mayor] Eddie [Espinoza] did to this village . . . ," she says, finishing her sentence with a shake of the head.

The trouble began in 2006, Skinner recalls, when Espinoza informed her that he was going to run against her for mayor. Espinoza had a very good chance of winning because "he knew everyone in town" by virtue of his job at Pancho Villa State Park in Columbus. When the votes were counted, Skinner had 100 and Espinoza had 190, making him the town's new mayor. Skinner didn't complain, because Columbus is a town of 1,600 people, most of whom are Hispanic and have close ties with family and friends in Palomas. "It's a Hispanic community. I'd rather have an Hispanic in as mayor. I really care about the people."

For the first few years, things seemed to run smoothly. But the economic downturn that gripped the country hit Columbus hard. "From 2007 and on there has been a real slowdown," Skinner says. Then the federal Environmental Protection Agency ordered the town to purify its water, which was naturally very high in arsenic and fluoride, saddling the town with debt because it had to install a reverse-osmosis water treatment system.

After Espinoza was reelected in 2010 by just nineteen votes, "things started to go downhill," Skinner says. When the town fire department landed a grant of $400,000, "He spent every penny of it." Vega collected a double salary as both the top police officer and the city manager. Inexplicably, the city hall was renovated and a new baseball field with lights was built. The city budget was quickly overspent, she says.

Skinner remains puzzled as to why the group became so involved in gunrunning, because the money was small compared to the risks. "I don't know why [they] would start in on the gun business. It wasn't as much money as you'd think. It never added up to me," which is why she suspects drugs may have been involved.

"Do you think the cartels were pressuring them to buy the guns?" I ask.

Skinner is skeptical about the cartel influence, since the town's gun smuggling was not on a large scale. "There's a lot of people who could [buy guns]" other than Espinoza, Vega, and Gutierrez, she says—and perhaps do it more effectively. "It was just an opportunity for these guys to make some money. It was small stuff. The cartels can buy anything they want. This was penny-ante stuff."

After the group was arrested, the town government ground to a halt. "We didn't know what to do for a while," she says. "We had to get [Espinoza] to resign [while] in prison. Blas [Gutierrez] was a town trustee. He had to resign also." The town's mayor pro tem, Roberto Gutierrez, the father of Blas Gutierrez, then nominated Nicole Lawson, one of the town's emergency medical technicians, as the new mayor.

"It's very sad," Skinner says of Columbus after the raid. The town's future is bleak, and it may have to dissolve. "It's a fun place to be, but we're not attracting any new folks. I don't see much going on here. The kids leave town because there are no jobs. Ghost towns become ghost towns for a reason."

## More Than Questionable

While the arrest of the gun ring rattled the town of Columbus, left to pick up the pieces is Mayor Lawson, whom I meet at the modest city hall in late October 2012. A young and soft-spoken woman, her calm exterior belies the chaos and confusion she faces trying to reassemble the city's accounts.

"It was all overspent," she says of the town budget, to the tune of about $700,000. She is still trying to figure out where all the money went. "They had gone through a one-year budget in the first three months." She has been coming across expense account entries of $90,000 for "miscellaneous." Emblems were removed from city vehicles and they were used for personal purposes; new uniforms and computers were purchased for city offices. "This went on from the time he was hired to the time he was arrested," Lawson says of the former mayor. "It was wasteful. We don't have money for that kind of thing." The few city employees remaining now scavenge for secondhand items to furnish the offices. "You make do," she says.

The town is delinquent in payments to the federal government and to the state's employee retirement association. Making those payments "is the only way we can bring the city up to standards," Lawson says. The city's "financial reports to the state were false." Because state and federal grant money was apparently misspent, "most want their money back. Columbus has shown that Columbus could not be trusted with the money." Lawson believes that some of the financial problems could have been averted if state auditors had alerted others in the town government. "It was more than questionable," she says of the expenditures. Now, the state is withholding approval of the town budget, and like former mayor Skinner, Lawson fears that Columbus may have to legally dissolve.

Lawson treasures the sense of community in Columbus. After a divorce, she joined her father, a former US Navy seaman who had retired to Columbus, and she worked as an EMT. Despite everything that's happened, she's not angry with Espinoza. "Eddie and I were friends. The community felt they were not being represented. Eddie got elected because he has very good ideas and was very passionate. Most people here have family on the other side of the border. That makes us feel close with Palomas." Lawson says she didn't have any connections with Columbus before moving there, but after a decade, "I learned what community can mean."

As an EMT, Lawson personally witnessed the spillover of cartel violence. Victims of cartel gun battles would stumble across the border, wounded and bleeding, and the town's medical team would be called. Some victims ran to the port of entry because Palomas' top doctor had been threatened by the cartel not to treat any of their shooting or beating victims or he, too, would be killed.

"We were getting men who were beaten with rifle butts and two-by-fours and told that they had two weeks to decide if they wanted to traffic [drugs] or this would happen to their family," Lawson says. In one case, a beating victim was worried sick about his family back in Palomas. "All he could talk about was his family and that they would rape his family and burn his house down if he didn't do what they wanted." Lawson pauses at the memory. "Then they stopped coming. I don't know what happened," she says, adding that many people fled Palomas.

In light of the drug violence that has hit both sides of the border and the arrests of the gun-smuggling ring, Lawson believes that federal agents involved in Fast and Furious should be held accountable for their actions, or lack of action. "I think Fast and Furious was a debacle. The government promoted gun trafficking and put guns in the hands of the cartels without a way of tracking them. Why aren't those men in jail?" she asks. "I don't think any of it was right."

Putting Columbus back together has become a full-time job, Lawson says, forcing her to quit her job as an EMT at night so she can work as mayor by day. The town has disbanded its police department and turned to the Luna County sheriff for security. Lawson has also closed city hall three days a week, saying, "We don't have the money" to be open any more than that. She is also looking to replace some key employees who have resigned or been fired, including the town clerk and treasurer. Despite the troubles, Lawson remains optimistic. "We've paid off a lot of our debt," she says, but adds, "There's a long way to go."

## Furniture and Hamburgers

Phillip Skinner, sixty-five, the brother of hotel owner Martha Skinner, runs a sandwich and burger shop out of a mobile home parked beside the road not far from the center of Columbus. He takes orders through a sliding glass window then asks his customers to come back after the fifteen minutes it takes for him to prepare the fries and burgers. Business has been slow. "It's ratcheted down," Skinner says. When he opened two years ago, he was bringing in about $2,000 a month. Now it's less than half that, and half his income goes back out the door in food and operational costs. "We're not making any money. The economy is not good."

Not long ago Skinner had a thriving furniture factory in Palomas, a business he started after moving to Columbus from Los Angeles some twenty-five years ago. He was in the furniture business in L.A., and like others at the time, he looked for ways to cut labor costs and overhead to stay competitive. "Things were moving offshore" as furniture makers sought cheap labor. Skinner was familiar with the area since his father had once worked in Las Cruces, New Mexico. "We explored here and discovered Palomas. It was not as intimidating as Tijuana or Juárez. You go because of lower labor costs, about 25 percent of what labor costs in the US." He bought a small, eight-hundred-square-foot house in Palomas, converted it into a furniture shop, and hired one employee. By 2007 he had a fifteen-thousand-square-foot factory and sixty employees who produced American country–style furniture.

"We had to train everybody," he says of the workforce. "A lot of them only had a sixth-grade education." Because the labor was inexpensive, "if there was a problem, I threw people at the problem." But some problems were beyond his control, such as the US economy, which collapsed in 2008. In 2007 Skinner had three hundred furniture stores around the United States that carried his products. "We went to zero," he says, because the bottom fell out of the retail furniture market. "They got hammered," he says of furniture stores. "They just kept going out of business." Chinese-made furniture filled the void, he says. "We couldn't, even being in Mexico, compete with the Chinese," because the Chinese could sell a finished product for less than it cost Skinner to produce something similar. "So we went to custom-made furniture. But it didn't catch on." In a tight economy, people weren't interested in buying heirloom pieces, Skinner says. "They didn't want it to last forever." The US furniture market has "pretty much gone to throwaway."

As the economy fell, cartel violence along the border rose, Skinner says, and he was forced to close his business. When a popular dentist in Palomas was kidnapped from his office and the Palomas mayor was killed, "It scared me," Skinner says. "To downsize was OK with me. I was scared down there. But did [the violence] directly affect us? No." If the drug violence had hit his factory, "I would have moved my office to Columbus. I would have gone [to Palomas] less frequently." In the end it was the lack of business, not the violence, that closed the factory doors. Skinner sold his Mexican property for a little less than he paid for it, then returned to Columbus and opened the sandwich shop. "I can't afford to retire," he says, "and don't want to."

Slow business in the sandwich shop leaves time to think about the past, and the bust of the Columbus gun ring weighs on him. "I was really bothered by it. What was shocking was that others weren't outraged. These people betrayed their community." Skinner pauses for a moment to fry a couple of hamburgers, add the trimmings, then wrap and bag them. Mayor Espinoza was nicknamed Bully, he says, and the name suited him. "He bullied people and they were intimidated. Even his friends. When [Police Chief] Vega was hired, people said, 'You'll be sorry.' Wrong people put wrong people around them."

The group bought and sold weapons for the excitement and profit, he suspects. "It was the thrill of it all. Power is intoxicating, and money is a strong motivator. I think they went into it freely." He pauses to ring up the sale. "It's the human condition. I take a biblical stance on things. The bad guys are thinking about bad things all the time. If you don't want problems, hire honest people."

## Sheriff Cobos

With the police department of Columbus gone, keeping an eye on crime in the surrounding borderlands and the scattered communities is the responsibility of Luna County sheriff Raymond Cobos. I find Cobos in his office in a one-story building in Deming, the county seat, about thirty-five miles north of Columbus. Cobos nods sympathetically when I tell him I'm researching border issues and immigration. For most Americans, he says, the US-Mexico border is "some sort of foggy place down there."

The exception is Phoenix, Cobos says, which has become part of the national debate over immigration reform and border security because of Arizona's law Senate Bill 1070. Arizona's Maricopa County, which includes the metropolitan area of Phoenix, has a population of about 3.8 million, more than three times that of the entire state of New Mexico, with a population of 1.2 million. By comparison, Luna County has a population of about thirty-one thousand, about half of whom are Hispanic, Cobos says.

"What happens in Maricopa County is vastly different than what happens in Luna County. We are not a destination for the undocumented people," Cobos says. "There is no big industry here." The county has a 30 percent unemployment rate, he says, and because of this has few immigration problems. "There is no chance for undocumented people to get any real good-paying jobs." The biggest employers are the school district, the federal government such as the Border Patrol, and city and county governments.

The county also is home to many big ranches, and what few jobs they offer are seasonal. Cobos says his office is "aware of the hiring of illegals" but does not go after them in any significant way. The labor issue is more of a problem in communities to the east and along the Rio Grande and in New Mexico's Estancia Valley, he says, where factories have been built and the area is covered with pecan groves and farms growing alfalfa, chilies, melons, and onions.

Cartel violence along the border surfaced in 2005, Cobos says, and soon border security towers and cameras were installed. Roads were graded to improve access to remote areas favored by smugglers. Beefed-up security was a financial windfall for his department, Cobos says, which received $1.3 million for new vehicles, communications equipment, overtime, and other expenses as part of Operation Stone Garden, a project by the Department of Homeland Security to enlist local law enforcement into border security. "They want us to use our authority for interdiction" of undocumented people, Cobos says. Now Cobos's men have been "cross-deputized" and can make arrests in neighboring Hidalgo County, the remote "boot heel" area of New Mexico that borders Arizona and is favored by smugglers.

The cartel violence that exploded in Palomas in 2005 was due to the fighting between the Juárez Cartel, which had controlled the Palomas *plaza*, and the Sinaloa Cartel, which wanted it. Several times a week at least two or three bodies would be dumped at the border, Cobos says. "It was like the Al Capone days" of the Prohibition Era in Chicago. The violence then expanded into abductions, some of which occurred in Columbus. "There have been a number of Columbus residents who have disappeared."

More than 420 students in the Columbus public schools live in Palomas and cross the border each day to attend school. Buses from the Columbus school district meet them at the port of entry, take them to elementary, middle, and high schools, and return them at the end of the day. Cobos calls them "anchor babies," since they tie Mexican families to the United States.

More than once, border violence has put the students in danger. Once sheriff's deputies were summoned to a gunfight at the port of entry just as the school buses were unloading. He ordered the students back on the buses because "I didn't want to send them into an ongoing gunfight." The buses are now equipped with radios so drivers can contact deputies the moment violence happens.

The drug cartels have infiltrated every part of society, Cobos says, including the schools. "Every little town along the border has had their officials killed or threatened," Cobos says. He and his deputies were "uninvited" to Mexican public schools after they conducted a series of antigang and antidrug classes. The cartels did not want US law officers telling Mexican children not to get involved in the drug trade, because students are ideal for bringing drugs into the United States and taking money out.

The cartels "are not stupid people . . . so why not use [students]?" Cobos asks. It's easy for a student to carry a couple of kilos of marijuana or cocaine in a backpack, and if they're caught, the charges filed against children are minimal compared to adults. "They're expendable, they're pawns," Cobos says. And if the cartel encounters reluctance to cooperate, they use "fear and force," telling students, "Don't bother coming back from school today. Your family will be dead," he says. "It's a corruptive process." If a student refuses, saying, "'I don't want any of this, I don't want to get involved,' they kill him. Multiply that story one hundred times." Cobos shakes his head at the damage done to Mexican society by the drug cartels. "I underestimated the capacity of the Mexican society to absorb this violence."

Luna County deputies have been forced to provide escorts for the ambulances that pick up those wounded at the border by cartel violence, because cartel shooters chase their targets across the border even as the victims are being treated. Cobos recalls one wounded man who drove a car across the border while sitting in the passenger seat because the driver and another in the backseat had been shot dead. "If we have a victim come across, we will do everything we can."

Despite past gunfights, Cobos is not worried about the violence spilling across the border in any significant way. "I don't believe that armed battalions of assassins are going to storm across the border" because trouble at the border is bad business for the cartels, he says. "Killing a border agent or a deputy does not get you money. What do you gain?"

Columbus is familiar territory for Cobos, who started his career as the sheriff's deputy posted there. He knew Mayor Espinoza, but the two were not particularly friendly. "We had different points of view.

He supported my opponents" in the sheriff elections. Cobos is disappointed with Espinoza and Chief Vega. "Those who have the capacity to change things don't and often slip back in the old ways."

Cobos says he was not surprised when Espinoza selected Vega as his police chief. "A crooked mayor needs a crooked police chief," he says. Espinoza was able to hire Vega, who had a range of short-term jobs in law enforcement prior to Columbus, Cobos says, because the town had gone through eight chiefs in just four years. With the hiring of Vega, "the cast of characters was there" to put the gunrunning ring in motion. The gun sales started slow, but "as time went on, [Vega] got confident."

Cobos became suspicious when his deputies stopped Vega in his police vehicle three or four times driving at very high speeds on back country roads very late at night and for no apparent reason. Vega was warned about his speeding and seemed to understand the message. "I didn't have any problems [with Vega] after that."

The problems, however, were just beginning. Cobos suspects that the drug cartels did, in fact, reach Espinoza, Vega, and Blas Gutierrez. "Corrupt local officials—why not?" he asks. "If you corrupt the head of the police department, no one is going to question them buying anything. It was a perfect cover. It's a lot easier than [cartels] coming across the border and killing people."

Cobos is acutely aware of the ties between people on both sides of the border, ties that go back generations. Cobos is the top law officer in Luna County and notes with pride that his grandfather fought with Pancho Villa's army and may have been involved in Villa's raid on Columbus in 1916.

Cobos says his grandfather tired of the Mexican revolution and abandoned Villa's army, sneaking home because "If they found [deserters], they would hang them." But because his grandfather had become a friend of the daughter of one of Villa's commanders, who pleaded on his behalf, he was allowed to return to Villa's ranks without punishment. Back in the army, his grandfather was assigned the job of collecting bodies off the battlefields. "It was refreshing to get that information," he says of his grandfather's life, and Cobos was later able to meet his grandfather's sister in Mexico.

## Three Cups of Fear

New Mexico state senator John Smith typifies Democrats one finds in the western border regions: a fiscal conservative and social liberal. I find Smith, a resident of Deming and the representative of Columbus, in his Deming office on a warm and sun-splashed day in October.

People and drugs have been moving across the border for years, Smith says. "We've been aware of this for seventy years," but he adds, "It was a different border back then. We knew there was a drug issue in the 1950s, but it didn't really surface until after the Vietnam War." That the public school system in Deming and Columbus now educates more than four hundred US-born students from Palomas is just one of the changes Smith has seen in his lifetime. "When I was in high school it was only four or five students [from Mexico]."

It is no secret, Smith says, that "some of those kids are the coyotes because their families are being threatened," and they carry drugs in their backpacks. "The retribution is terrible," he says of a refusal to cooperate with the cartels. "The young kids live in fear. We've had some young people disappear and are found later murdered. It's been going on for twenty years." Smith says that school district officials didn't want drug-sniffing dogs in the school, because of the oppressive atmosphere it creates. "The common Mexican folks are fearful and the people on this side are fearful," he says. "We have a common thread here. You have fear along the border."

Smith dismisses the criticism leveled against the school district for continuing to educate students who live across the border in Palomas, saying that the more educated people there are on both sides of the border, the better. "I want to live next to an educated neighbor, not an uneducated one. We hope assimilation occurs, but we've had to take a step back" because of the corrupting influence of the drug cartels.

For decades people from Mexico migrated north seeking a better life. "Those people were escaping for better economic opportunities," Smith says. "Now they're escaping the drug cartels." Smith thinks that the estimated twelve million undocumented Mexicans living in the

United States may be an exaggeration, perhaps double the true figure, but it is used to justify the expenditure of some $25 billion to build up US-Mexico border security. In the 1960s, he says, there were just seven or eight Border Patrol officers in his district, and now there are about four hundred. The pervasive presence of the Border Patrol has contributed to the siege mentality along the border, he says. "Interdiction [of undocumented migrants] has been enhanced, but I'm not sure it has impeded the drugs coming across."

Better use of the area's ranchers would help with border security, Smith says, because ranchers are "the best eyes you have out there" and know their land better than anyone. But like many people, the ranchers are scared. "Ranchers won't talk on their cell phones" because they're afraid of being tracked and intercepted. Better border enforcement in the El Paso area east of Luna Country and along the Arizona border to the west has pushed drug smugglers into the southwestern corner of New Mexico that is Hidalgo County. "That boot heel is a real drug route. If you enforce the border in Arizona, you push them this way," he says of the smugglers. Though the number of drug interdictions may not be high compared to elsewhere, Smith says, "in relation to our numbers, the incidents are significant."

Smith longs for the days when people moved freely across the border and enjoyed themselves in Palomas. "We didn't have a lot of fear … when I was young." But that changed with cartel violence. He chafes at being unable to cross the border for fear of kidnapping because of his position as a senior member of the state legislature and committee chairman. "I don't like being a prisoner in my own community."

Smith agonizes over restrictive immigration laws that hamper the area's best students from pursing higher education. "Some of the best students we have are from across the border." If top students are denied educational opportunities, they may succumb to the lure of criminal enterprises. "The money temptation is strong in high-poverty areas," he says. "The temptation is strong to move those drugs."

Solving the border crisis also means reducing the massive American demand for drugs, Smith says. "You've got to reduce the demand here." Otherwise, "It will be fifty years before things improve."

## The Pink Store

A couple of days later, I park my car in the small lot at the Columbus port of entry and walk across the border into Palomas, following a man rolling himself along in a well-worn wheelchair. As in most border towns, the first shops encountered are a mix of video stores, taco stands, auto parts stores, and dental offices. Another block in and across the street is a two-story, bright pink building known as the Pink Store. It's a Palomas landmark where one can dine on fine Mexican food, enjoy a variety of Mexican beer and tequila cocktails, and buy Mexican pottery, arts and crafts, and tax-free alcohol.

At the counter, I ask for the proprietors, Ivonne and Sergio Romero. The young woman frowns at first, wondering who I am and what I want, then smiles and says, "I'm Ivonne." She calls her husband and guides me to a table at the edge of the restaurant's dining room.

For two generations the Pink Store has been one of the region's most popular tourist spots. But business has lagged because of what Ivonne calls a "domino effect." First, passports were required of Americans who wanted to visit Mexico, not to enter Mexico but to get back into the United States. Then the economy collapsed, followed by the rise in cartel violence that affected all of the border communities. In 2009 the swine flu outbreak was traced to a small village in Mexico, and "people started covering their faces with masks," Ivonne says.

As news spread of the cartel killings in cities from Tijuana to Juárez, the fear factor rose. "People stopped coming. For a while, a lot of things were closed." But the bad news did not reflect the reality of day-to-day life, Ivonne insists. "I have never been threatened or anything. Do we quit living because things happen?" The store's most committed customers continue to visit. "We have a lot of repeat business. A lot of people never quit coming."

The mood along the US-Mexico border changed following the al-Qaeda attacks of 9/11, Ivonne says, but notes, "That was in New York." Terrorism was never a problem along the border, yet following 9/11, the border became a threat, she says, and the security response has been excessive and perhaps unnecessary.

"But the dangers in Palomas were real," I say, mentioning the cartel killings.

"If I feel threatened or sense there is danger," Ivonne concedes, she can leave. "I have a plan. We can load up all the stuff [in the store] and sell it elsewhere." She admits that the cartel killings bothered her. "At that point, I felt what I hadn't felt before," but still, it did not deter her or her husband. "You just can't stop. You keep going and you share what you have."

Members of her family have left not because of the violence, but for economic reasons, because some maquiladora plants have closed. The closings created "a floating community of workers," Ivonne explains, who came to the border factories for work. When the plants closed, many crossed into the United States and abandoned their children in Palomas. "The hardest thing is the children who have been left without parents."

Ivonne's husband, Sergio, is confident that the worst has passed. Tour buses are starting to return and business is up by nearly 30 percent. "It's coming," he says of resurgent business. "We've never had a big problem [with security]. We chose not to live in fear. It's about being present" and focusing on the tasks at hand.

The climate of fear on the border has hurt both countries, Ivonne says. "The whole fence thing was a waste of money. There is tragedy in all of this. Hopefully it will make us stronger as a community."

"If [the United States] needs people to work, then open it up," Sergio says of the border.

The cross-border ties in Columbus and elsewhere along the border run long and deep. Few people are happy about how life in the borderlands has changed and how a climate of fear now hovers over the region. There are deep roots to the life and lore along the border, as I will soon find out.

# 8

# THE GHOST OF PANCHO VILLA

☀

**A**s a reporter in the late 1980s for the *New Mexican*, Santa Fe's daily newspaper, I treasured any opportunity to get out of the newsroom to cover a good story. When a handful of activists armed and barricaded themselves on a parcel of land not far from the northern New Mexico town of Tierra Amarilla, I jumped at the chance. The town's name means "yellow land," from the color of the fall foliage, and it is the seat of Rio Arriba County government. As I drove north from Santa Fe, I had no idea I was about to enter a world of lingering Hispanic resentment and territorial strife that gurgles below the surface of daily life in parts of the American Southwest. It is a resentment born of America's largely forgotten conquest of Mexico in 1848.

The twentieth-century land grant protest I encountered in Tierra Amarilla in 1987 caught most people by surprise, even though it echoed a similar and violent event that occurred in the town twenty years before. As anti–Vietnam War protests roiled across the United States in the late 1960s and as African American and Hispanic activism was on the rise, the Alianza Federal de Mercedes (Federal Alliance of Land Grants) surfaced, led by Reies López Tijerina. A radicalized Texas transplant, Tijerina organized a series of confrontations with authorities to draw attention to the loss of lands granted to individuals and groups by the governments of Spain and of Mexico. Initiated by the Spanish crown, the practice had continued after Mexico won independence from Spain in 1821 to encourage Mexicans to settle the vast and largely uncolonized northern provinces that are now Texas, New Mexico, Colorado, Arizona, Utah, Nevada, and California.

Nowhere had the land grant issue become as contentious as in New Mexico, one of the most impoverished states in the United States, where land and life were profoundly linked. Many of the heirs of the original grantees of the 1832 Tierra Amarilla Land Grant continued to live on or near former land grant property, which over the years had ended up in the hands of private, often out-of-state developers, or the federal government. The protestors said the heirs had been cheated out of what was rightfully theirs.

The Alianza protests in October 1966 included the occupation of a US Forest Service campground in a rock formation in northern New Mexico called the Echo Amphitheater. A former colleague from the *Albuquerque Journal*, Larry Calloway, was covering Tijerina and the protests at the time. In his personal blog post on the fortieth anniversary of the Tierra Amarilla raid (http://larrycalloway.com/courthouse-raid), Calloway wrote about the protest and the charismatic Tijerina, whom he described as a "fiery" orator who could play to the lingering resentments of the land grantee descendants.

On June 5, 1967, while filing a story about a bond hearing for members of the Alianza at the Rio Arriba County Courthouse pay phone, Calloway found himself in the midst of an armed assault. The reason for the raid, Calloway wrote, was that the Santa Fe district attorney had obtained arrest warrants for leaders of the Alianza to prevent a planned "unlawful assembly." Police had arrested some members of the group, including Tijerina's brother, and they were brought to a hearing where their bond was set.

Tijerina saw the hearing as an opportunity to challenge the legitimacy of the government and the legal system that had stripped the heirs of their property. That day, about twenty Alianza members armed themselves and gathered south of Tierra Amarilla, then drove to the courthouse, where Tijerina planned to make a citizen's arrest of the district attorney. But the DA wasn't there, having sent his assistant,

who slipped away after the district court judge released the six defendants. The armed Alianza members arrived shortly after the hearing
ended, just as Calloway was on the pay phone:

> The first shot was fired just behind me in the hall of the Rio
> Arriba County Courthouse. I was telephoning a news story
> to my editor in Albuquerque. I whipped around, saw a drawn
> pistol and dropped to the floor of the five-foot-long telephone
> booth.
>
> "Some guy just took a shot at someone," I said over the
> long-distance wires.
>
> "Who was it?"
>
> "I don't know. I'm on the floor. They'll get him in a minute."
>
> A state police officer had been standing in the hall just a
> few feet away and the sheriff and two deputies were in an open
> office next to the telephone booth. I raised up, expecting to see
> the officers handcuffing whoever had fired the shot, but instead
> I saw all hell break loose. Armed men in work clothes or Army
> fatigues were storming into the hall. I hit the floor again.
>
> "It's a raid! I'm scared as hell."
>
> Then the whole town seemed to explode with gunshots.
> I tossed the receiver to the back of the booth and flattened
> myself against the wall. The editor counted eight rapid shots
> before the phone went dead.
>
> There was more shooting in the sheriff's office, then I heard
> the regular bursts of a machine gun outside. I could hear the
> moans of a badly wounded man in the hall. I had no idea how
> many others had been shot. Somebody was thrown against
> the phone booth door and slid to the floor, holding the bro-
> ken door shut. I heard the machine gun firing upstairs in the
> courtroom. . . .

The National Guard was sent to Tierra Amarilla, and Calloway, who
was taken by the group, eventually escaped at a state police roadblock.

Members of the Alianza were subsequently arrested and put on trial. There were few convictions, despite the shooting of a state patrolman and the death, apparently from a beating, of a sheriff's deputy. Tijerina successfully defended himself, convincing an Albuquerque jury that he was innocent of all charges. Tijerina was later found guilty of federal charges and spent three years in prison.

I did not know what to expect when I drove up to Tierra Amarilla. I had made contact with some friends and supporters of the protestors, and had been assured that I would be safe. I planned to spend a day and a night with the group, then return and write my story. I spoke with the state police press officer and told him what I was going to do. He didn't say explicitly what the state police planned, but it was clear that they were prepared to send in a SWAT team should the situation get out of hand. I was going in at my own risk.

Apparently because of the mayhem of the courthouse raid twenty years earlier, local and state police and government officials were taking a low-key approach to this new protest. As I traveled north through Tierra Amarilla, not a police officer was in sight. It was as if the protest was not happening. I crested a hill, turned off the road, and parked at a fence gate where the protest was marked by a poster that proclaimed TIERRA O MUERTO ("Land or Death") and depicted a black-and-white image of a heavily mustachioed Pancho Villa wearing a large sombrero, grasping a carbine, and resting his hand on a sword handle. It was sunny and quiet. I waited, and soon someone came running, opened the gate, and I was in.

The protest was led by Pedro Archuleta, a stocky and articulate man, who was accompanied by several other men and women. For the most part, the group stayed in a small mobile home that had been hauled onto the land. A latrine had been dug, and cooking was done in a makeshift outdoor kitchen. Meals were taken outside around a campfire. The weapons I saw included a few hunting rifles and several semiautomatic pistols.

Ironically, the man for whom this protest was being conducted, Amador Flores, was absent. Flores had filed a claim to about 250 acres of land that records showed was owned by Arizona speculators. When Flores refused to leave, he was reportedly jailed, prompting the protest.

The camp consisted of only a few acres of the disputed parcel, which Archuleta declined to show me, fearing a police ambush if he wandered too far afield. He had created a perimeter to the camp that was patrolled every hour or so by one or another of the protestors. At various spots along the circular path, the group had built bunkers of dirt and pine logs from which defenders could shoot through narrow openings. Archuleta also had built a military-styled obstacle course, explaining that he didn't want the group to get soft.

There was not much to do at the camp, so I had time to talk with Archuleta and the others. In fact, it felt less like a protest than a camping trip, except for occasional bouts of fear and paranoia that Archuleta injected into the conversation. Once or twice each day, a local state trooper or sheriff's deputy would pull up to the gate, and he and Archuleta would talk amiably, as if discussing the weather, then the officer would drive away. Others in the camp came and went at will, often bringing back supplies. Cars and trucks passed on the highway as if nothing strange was happening.

It was during one of the extended conversations with Archuleta when I learned about the Treaty of Guadalupe Hidalgo, the document that settled the Mexican-American War of 1846–48 and ceded to the United States all of Mexico's vast northern provinces, the wide expanse of territory from California to Texas that became the American Southwest. I knew of the treaty in name only and had no knowledge of its significance. I recalled nothing about the treaty or the Mexican-American War from my high school US history classes, which may reflect on my poor scholarship at the time, if not the "other world" attitude Americans have of the Southwest.

## War with Mexico

The Mexican-American War and the treaty that ended it loomed large over this protest outside of Tierra Amarilla, as well as other locations in

New Mexico where large Mexican land grants had once existed. Mexico achieved independence in 1821, at a time when the United States was rapidly expanding westward across the continent and fulfilling its "manifest destiny." In 1803 the United States acquired the Louisiana Purchase, some 828,000 square miles of land from France, for about $15 million in cash and debt cancellation. The territory covered all or parts of what are now fourteen US states: Arkansas, Missouri, Iowa, Oklahoma, Kansas, Nebraska, Minnesota, North and South Dakota, northeastern New Mexico, northern Texas, as well as eastern portions of Montana, Wyoming, and Colorado.

In a highly readable account of the war titled *A Glorious Defeat: Mexico and Its War with the United States*, by professor of history Timothy Henderson of Auburn University, at the time of Mexico's independence, people such as Stephen Austin were selling vast amounts of land in the territory of Texas to American settlers searching for new opportunities. Along with the rest of what would become the American Southwest, Texas belonged to Mexico and for the previous three hundred years had belonged to Spain, dating from the conquest of the Aztec empire by the Spanish explorer Hernán Cortés. Mexico permitted the influx of Americans into Texas because Austin had pledged allegiance to Mexico, knowing that without it, his right to sell land was a fiction. Although Mexican officials had misgivings about their permission, they were also having a hard time encouraging their own citizens to migrate north.

Mexico's suspicions that America had its eyes on Texas began to materialize by the 1830s, when Texans began to clamor for autonomy from Mexican taxes, rules, and regulations. Finally, in 1835, an army of Texans drove the Mexican Army out of the territory and then withdrew, leaving about one hundred of their fellow Texans to man the Alamo fortress in San Antonio. These defenders were eventually joined by notorious characters such as James Bowie, namesake of the Bowie knife, and David "Davy" Crockett, the frontiersman and former three-time congressman who became an American folk hero.

In early 1836 Mexican General Antonio López de Santa Anna gathered an army of five thousand men to retake the Texas territory. In early March, Santa Ana attacked the Alamo with fifteen hundred soldiers, killing everyone there. Angered by Santa Anna's take-no-prisoners tactics, the Texans responded by crushing Santa Anna's army in the Battle of San Jacinto a month later. Santa Anna's defeat concluded the Texas revolt and created the short-lived Republic of Texas.

The borderline between Texas and Mexico was left unsettled, however. Texas claimed it was the Rio Grande, not the line much more to the east that the Mexicans had insisted. Mexico never recognized Texas as an independent country because of the border dispute, but the United States did. Nearly a decade passed before the States annexed Texas all the way to the Rio Grande, and to enforce it, sent an army led by General Zachary Taylor to Corpus Christi, Texas. So began the inevitable slide into war.

When the United States declared war on Mexico on May 13, 1846, a cavalry force under General Stephen W. Kearny rode into New Mexico, quickly taking the garrisons and government center in Santa Fe and moving on to El Paso. Kearny pushed westward to California, where he met with John C. Frémont and the California Battalion, which had defeated the Mexican forces assigned to what was then called Alta California.

US naval ships took up positions on Mexico's Pacific coast, because the United States worried that Britain might try to interfere with America's military plans. Yet another US force under Taylor's command drove south into Mexico from Texas and then west to take the northern Mexican city of Monterrey.

Rather than reinforcing Taylor's army as the war dragged into 1847, President James K. Polk sent a separate force commanded by General Winfield Scott that stormed ashore near Mexico's east coast port of Veracruz in March 1847 and began a drive to Mexico City. It was the first major amphibious landing of American forces in US history. The force of twelve thousand volunteer and regular soldiers included men who would later play key roles in the American Civil War: Robert E. Lee, Ulysses S. Grant, and Thomas "Stonewall" Jackson.

By September 1847 Scott's army was in Mexico City and attacked the strategic Chapultepec Castle; within days it fell. Among the legacies of the Mexican-American War is the opening line of the US Marines' hymn, "From the halls of Montezuma . . . ," which refers to the marines who died storming the castle. The defeated Mexican Army was led once again by Santa Anna. In the final battle, however, Mexico found its own heroes. Six military cadets aged thirteen to nineteen refused to fall back when ordered to retreat, and fought to the death. According to legend, the last of the six wrapped himself in the Mexican flag and jumped off the castle rather than be taken prisoner. A monument was built to them.

Signed on February 2, 1848, at the town of Guadalupe Hidalgo, the treaty ceded to the United States what is now the American Southwest. In compensation for the land, the United States agreed to assume about $3 million in claims US citizens said they were owed by the Mexican government, and pay Mexico $15 million for the vast territory. When the US Senate ratified the treaty, however, it removed the article that stated the United States would recognize the land grants that had been awarded by the Spanish crown and the Mexican government.

The final changes to the US-Mexico border came six years later in 1854, when the United States bought what was known as the Gadsden Purchase for $10 million. The land totaled some forty-five thousand square miles and included what is now the southwestern portion of New Mexico and most of southern Arizona. The deal was struck in large part because Santa Anna, despite his defeats, had become the leader of Mexico and needed the money.

## In the Land Grant Camp

Wars had been fought and treaties had been signed more than 120 years earlier, yet the aftereffects of the long history between Mexico and the United States were still being felt in the mountains of northern New

Mexico. That night in the camp outside of Tierra Amarilla, Archuleta told me if I was to stay in the camp, I had to participate in camp life. As we prepared for bed, he explained that meant walking guard duty. This didn't worry me, since it meant a short trek in the dark around the well-worn perimeter path. I might stumble across a skunk, I thought, or at worst a police SWAT team in dark camouflage and face paint. If the latter, I'd quietly walk away.

Archuleta woke me at the designated hour to walk the perimeter and handed me a .45-caliber pistol in a holster attached to a thick web belt. I balked, knowing this meant crossing the line of journalistic impartiality. I explained my predicament, but Archuleta insisted, saying that he had walked guard duty several times that night, since others had left the camp. He needed to sleep. To walk the perimeter without a weapon would compromise camp security, he said. I badly wanted to write a complete story about the camp, and walking the perimeter was part of it. I didn't feel compromised and would never use the weapon, even on a skunk. I took it and made the walk.

It was a bad decision, of course—the story was killed because of it. I took little satisfaction knowing that there would be many other stories to write. The camp protest near Tierra Amarilla continued for months and died a quiet death. The Arizona landowners later deeded Flores a piece of land and apparently sold the rest, ridding themselves of a headache.

## The First Raid on Columbus

Twenty-five years after my escapade in Tierra Amarilla, I am in Columbus, New Mexico, and reminded that America's contentious relationship with Mexico did not end with the Mexican-American War. That fact is abundantly clear as I walk the creaky wooden floors of the Columbus Historical Museum, housed in the town's old and high-ceilinged train station. The museum is dedicated to the March 9, 1916, raid on Columbus by the revolutionary Francisco "Pancho" Villa that destroyed part of the town nearly a hundred years ago.

The drama of Villa's attack is prominently displayed across repro-
ductions of the front page of the March 9, 1916, edition of the *Santa
Fe New Mexican* newspaper, which are available at the museum. VILLA
INVADES THE U.S., the headline shouts, and under that, "Bandits Burn
and Kill in Columbus." Datelined Columbus, NM, the story reads:

> A band of Mexican bandits, numbering from 800 to 1,000,
> supposedly under the personal command of Francisco Villa,
> raided the United States territory, early today. They killed
> American civilians who exposed themselves and set fire to
> several buildings. For nearly two hours the fighting continued
> in the streets. Col. H.J. Slocum brought the Thirteenth Cavalry
> into action and shortly after six o'clock drove the raiders back
> across the border. Eight civilians and six United States troop-
> ers were known dead early today. While the only word given
> out was that steps would be taken to punish the Villa bandits,
> it was not indicated whether [Mexican] General [Venustiano]
> Carranza would be called upon to do so, or whether Ameri-
> can troops would be sent over the line. Later American troops
> crossed the line in pursuit.

While the main headline and first sentences tell the story, other
headlines illustrate the burning anti-Mexican fervor that erupted
over the raid and fanned the flames of animosity. One reads, "DEATH
TO AMERICANS" PANCHO'S CRY; WANT TO CHOKE HATED GRINGO,
and the subheadline is even more graphic: "Villa, Personally Leading Attack to Force International War, Threatens to Make Torch Out
of Every Man, Woman and Child; Would Make Mexico 'Stick In our
Throats' When We Swallow It; Lays Blame on America For Present
Plight of His Country." Yet another is just as lurid: AMERICAN TORN
FROM WIFE'S ARMS, SHOT LIKE A DOG AND ROASTED, and below
it more details are offered: "American Citizens on American Soil
Enticed From Homes by Blood-Mad Torch-Squad of Mexican Brutes
and Shot Down; Murderers Laugh at Woman's Frantic Appeals for

Mercy; Bandits Go Through Hotel Firing into Rooms at Defenseless Occupants."

The very next day, President Woodrow Wilson ordered a "punitive" expedition into Mexico with the sole purpose of capturing Villa "dead or alive." Wilson made it clear that the army being sent was "friendly aid" and the mission was to be done with "scrupulous respect for the sovereignty of that republic." The expedition would be led by Gen. John J. "Black Jack" Pershing, who commanded Fort Bliss in El Paso and who would later command US forces in Europe in World War I.

Villa attacked the United States even though about ten thousand US soldiers were already stationed along the US-Mexico border from Douglas, Arizona, to El Paso, Texas, and about a third were cavalry. This substantial number of troops had been amassed because of Villa and the Mexican revolution that had been raging since 1910. The substantial presence of US military in the early twentieth century set a precedent for the contemporary borderlands.

Pershing's punitive expedition, which employed America's first air force, continued for about ten months but ended in failure. Villa was never found, and only about two hundred or so of Villa's army were killed or captured. The search for Villa ended rather quietly when Pershing was recalled to Washington, DC, as America prepared to enter World War I, which it did formally in April 1917.

The question remains as to why Villa conducted the raid, knowing that it would infuriate the United States and draw a response far beyond the ability of his ragtag army of Villistas to repulse. But clues to the attack, which is still debated by historians, appear in the newspaper reports of the day. According to a March 10, 1916, story in the *Santa Fe New Mexican* and datelined Columbus, a letter dated January 6, 1916, and written by Villa to his fellow revolutionary Emiliano Zapata, was captured in the battle at Columbus. In it Villa writes of his weariness of the revolution and suggests that Mexico should turn its attention to the north. He asks Zapata, who controlled southern Mexico, to join him in an attack on the United States. "I shall not expend another shell on brother Mexicans," Villa reportedly wrote, "but will prepare and organize to attack the Americans on their own soil and let them know that Mexico is a land of the free and the tomb of the traitors."

At the time, Villa, Zapata, and Venustiano Carranza, along with several other key leaders, had been fighting the revolution since 1910. After defeating the forces of the former longtime dictator President Porfirio Díaz, the revolutionaries had struggled among themselves for power. After anxiously watching the twists and turns of the Mexican revolution, President Wilson ultimately recognized Carranza as the legitimate leader of Mexico, believing that Carranza, a well-educated man, was the country's best hope for the future.

Wilson also put restrictions on Villa, who for years had been buying supplies, weapons, and horses in the United States and had assisted Carranza's forces in defeating Villa in a battle at the town of Agua Prieta, just across the border at Douglas, Arizona. Now that Villa was cut off, and having been handed a stinging defeat at the hands of his archrival, Villa was isolated and desperate. In that same letter, Villa revealed his anger at the United States and accused Carranza of selling out Mexico to the Americans.

Villa vented his anger by conducting his own punitive raid on Columbus, and thereby showed that he was unafraid of either Carranza or the United States. In reality Villa's power was declining, and with General Pershing on his trail, Villa was put on the defensive and ultimately took a secondary role in the aftermath of the revolution. Villa survived Pershing's expedition and eventually retired on a military pension. He died at the age of forty-five in July 1923 at the hands of assassins.

Lingering resentment over Mexico's concession of its former northern provinces continued to play a role in US-Mexico relations. This role was no more prominent than in America's entry into World War I, which came less than a year after Villa's raid on Columbus. On January 16, 1917, a telegram was written by German foreign secretary Arthur Zimmermann and sent via the German ambassador to the Mexican president. The telegram, which was intercepted and deciphered by

British intelligence, asked the Mexican government to join Germany in the war should the United States enter World War I on the side of Britain and France.

In exchange, Germany promised massive aid so that Mexico could reconquer some of its ceded land from the United States. The text of the telegram read in part: "We make Mexico a proposal of alliance on the following basis: make war together, make peace together, generous financial support and an understanding on our part that Mexico is to reconquer the lost territory in Texas, New Mexico, and Arizona." When the contents of what was known as the Zimmermann Telegram became public, the American public was outraged, propelling the United States to enter World War I on the side of Britain and France.

The telegram came almost seventy years after the Treaty of Guadalupe Hidalgo had been signed yet had appealed to Mexico's resentment of its past defeats by the US Army and the sale of its territories. America's virulent response to the telegram, which some at the time said was tantamount to an act of war, not only embroiled the United States in a bloody war on the European continent but also underscored America's profound conviction that the Southwest, from Texas to California, was and would remain US soil. The divergent sentiments on both sides of the border continue to roil, as I would soon learn.

## Gone but Not Forgotten

Though the ghosts of Villa's raid on Columbus may be blotted out by the sunlight, one can sense their presence in the calm and quiet of the Columbus Historical Museum. Under a glass case is a painted death mask of Pancho Villa. Artifacts, weapons, and photographs cover the walls. Like pieces of a jigsaw puzzle, together they tell of that infamous day that is slowly fading into the dusty halls of history.

For Richard Dean, great-grandson of one of the victims of Villa's raid, that day still lives. His ancestor, James T. Dean, ran a general store in Columbus and was killed in the raid. "When the shooting started, it woke [the family]," Dean tells me as we sit on a couple of rickety railroad chairs in a quiet corner of the museum. Much of what he recalls is family lore, passed on through generations, including his great-grandmother, who survived the raid. James kept an eye on the fighting that morning by frequently peeking out the backdoor. As many of the buildings in town were burning, residents tried to put out the fires, despite the shooting. "He wanted to go downtown to help put out the fires," Dean says. "That's where they found his body, on Main Street."

Dean's great-uncle, Edwin, who was James's son and about twenty at the time, was also anxious to join the fray and went to find a weapon and ammunition. As he ran down the street, however, Edwin came face-to-face with a Villista, who took aim and fired. "He felt the bullet go by his ear," Dean recalls being told. Edwin, who lived to be ninety-six, explained, "It was at that time I determined that my presence was needed elsewhere," Dean says, then adds, "That's the way he talked." Edwin eventually joined a force of volunteers who chased the Villistas deep into Mexico.

The carnage left in the streets was extensive, Dean says of the aftermath. "Dead horses and Villistas were all over the place." By some accounts, Villa may have lost seventy-five men that day. "Everyone who had a wagon or a team of horses was brought in. Bodies were piled outside of town and burned." Edwin found his brother's body as the dead were being collected from the streets, and sadly informed the family, "They got Papa." A morgue was set up in the Columbus State Bank, and Dean's great-grandmother took shelter in the city's school-house for several days. After the raid, the Dean family continued to operate the general store, he says, since Columbus was flooded with soldiers and airmen. "The general store did a booming business when the army was there."

A forgotten aspect of Pershing's expedition, Dean says, is that America's fledgling air force was brought to Columbus to provide aerial surveillance for US troops. Within days of the Villa raid, eight Curtiss biplanes from the US Army's 1st Aero Squadron were flown from San Antonio, Texas, to a makeshift airfield at Columbus. The army had purchased its first airplane, the Wright Flyer, some seven years earlier. Within weeks of arriving in New Mexico, however, most of the biplanes were damaged because of mechanical problems and the rough terrain and winds.

"A takeoff was an adventure," Dean says, "and a landing was a crash. The winds were unbearable." The airplanes couldn't cope with the strong gusts and the violent drafts of the nearby ten-thousand-foot Sierra Madre Mountains, where Villa and his men were hiding. "They couldn't get over the hills," Dean says of the underpowered planes. "None of the pilots were killed, which was amazing to me."

According to one account, three pilots were forced to land outside Chihuahua City and were soon surrounded by an angry mob of Villa supporters who destroyed the wood-and-fabric aircraft. "They were crazy or brave," Dean says of the pilots. "This was a total learning experience for the military." The American pilots learned from their troubles in the search for Villa and were better equipped and prepared when they entered World War I in France in 1917.

When the US Army left Columbus in 1925, it "became a ghost town," Dean says. "My family left," eventually selling the homestead in 1941. A former resident of the San Francisco Bay area, Dean and his wife returned to Columbus "to find my grandfather's grave. We met a lot of really nice people," and returned for the annual March celebration of Villa's raid, finally settling in Columbus.

Dean has seen a lot of changes in the town. "There are more people here who we don't know, and they don't want to be known," he says. "It's the drug thing. We don't go to Palomas any more than we have to," which is mostly for the inexpensive dental work and optical supplies. "It's not like before. We don't know what's going on there."

Dean lives on ten acres outside of town and is happy for the substantial presence of the Border Patrol. "We had groups of as many as twenty people with children" walking across his property, migrants who had just crossed the border. They occasionally stopped for water, he says, and "were looking for work." Much of the immigration seems to have slowed in the past couple of years. "We seldom see any coming across anymore." Yet in the rugged Tres Hermanas Mountains behind his house, Dean knows of trails littered with bottles and backpacks left by migrants. He suspects that he now sees fewer people crossing not because of better enforcement but because "they're getting better at concealing themselves."

Dean supports immigration reform and thinks the United States should reinstate what was called the Bracero Program, which granted temporary work visas to Mexicans. "It worked great. Why can't they take something that worked and build on that? It's beyond me. Times change so the program has to change."

The day after talking with Dean, I leave Columbus for southern Arizona, where I meet with ardent advocates of increased security enforcement along the US-Mexico border. Among them is Glenn Spencer, the man whom I'd met in the border security exposition in El Paso.

# IV

★ ★ ★

# THE ENFORCERS

# 9

# GUARDIANS OF THE BORDER

❁

**From his land in southern Arizona,** Glenn Spencer points across the US-Mexico border to a broken-down corral. It was once owned by the famed movie actor John Wayne, Spencer says, who raised horses and cattle in Mexico and sold them from that spot when the fence separating the two countries was just barbed wire. Today the border fence is a formidable barrier of eighteen-foot-high rusted steel and concrete-filled posts flanked by a graded and graveled road frequented by the ubiquitous green and white Border Patrol vehicles.

Spencer has spent many an evening watching that corral and the dilapidated buildings beside it, explaining that it's a staging area for Mexican migrants to cross the border. The fence is virtually impenetrable, Spencer says, but stops just short of the riverbed at the corner of his property. That's where the crossings are made, he says with a wave of his arm. Migrants wait until dark and walk along the river into the United States, hiding in the thick brush along the banks.

He has watched the border with a thermal, infrared camera and tracked the movement of many who have made the crossing. "In six months, we aided in the apprehension of sixteen hundred people and the shipments of drugs," Spencer boasts. He posted the images on the Internet to prove that the US-Mexico border is far from secure, despite the proclamations to the contrary by the US Border Patrol. "Then they put a fence in, and it all stopped," or so the government contends, he says with cynicism. In reality, the crossings were redirected to the fence gap at the river and to trails to the west that wind into the nearby Huachuca Mountains.

"They're not interested in securing the border," Spencer says of the government. "They make it look like they're doing something, but they're not." Because the border is not secure, those responsible are "guilty of negligence and malfeasance" in office, he says. Spencer has been fighting to secure the border for more than two decades. "I've watched crazy for twenty years," he says with a weak smile. "That's why I'm crazy." There is a larger mission to the struggle, Spencer says, and it is the integrity of America. "If we don't have a border, we don't have a country." Without a border, he asks, "then who is a citizen? How do we decide?"

Spencer takes me to one of two enormous plywood panels painted bright blue and decorated with thousands of miniature US flags. The flags are arranged so they spell out the words SECURE THE BORDER. "People ask if I'm doing this alone," he says, gesturing to the wall. "There are twenty thousand flags here from people who want to secure our borders."

To the consternation of the US Border Patrol, Spencer has a couple of small aircraft housed in an outbuilding. One is a small unmanned aerial surveillance plane that he calls the *Border Hawk*, which carries a camera that relays pictures to his computerized command center. He has used it to help the Border Patrol find intruders, he says. The Border Patrol made him ground the device. For a while Spencer also flew his own ultralight aircraft up and down the border, not only to spot illegal crossings but to keep an eye on the Border Patrol. The Border Patrol grounded that as well, claiming it interfered with their work.

Spencer is one of the most visible and vocal gadflies in the movement to seal America's borders to illegal immigration. In 2002 Spencer founded an organization called the American Border Patrol, of which he is president, according to the group's website, www.americanborderpatrol.com. Born and raised in California, Spencer received a degree in economics and mathematics and in the 1970s became involved in real estate and natural resource development, including geothermal energy development in Northern California. He formed a company with two Native Americans called Arrowstar Inc., a seismic oil exploration company that landed contracts with several major oil companies. The company found oil deposits in Montana and North Dakota. It is that same ground sensing technology that Spencer adapted to the seismic border crossing detection systems he promoted at the border technology conference in El Paso.

In the late 1980s Spencer became obsessed with illegal immigration and in 1992 formed Voice of Citizens Together, also known in California as the American Patrol, according to the Southern Poverty Law Center (SPLC). Spencer was a primary backer in 1994 of California's controversial Proposition 187, which would have required police, health care professionals, and teachers to check the immigration status of anyone of any age who was receiving public benefits, from education to health care. It would have prohibited the children of undocumented immigrants from attending public schools or receiving public health services.

Spencer was a regular on various Southern California news media outlets, urging the arrest and deportation of all undocumented people and the banning of foreign-language TV and radio. He suggested that Latinos and blacks were more prone to crime than other ethnic and racial groups and raised an alarm about the Aztlán Reconquista theory, according to the SPLC, which espoused that Mexico was plotting to reclaim its lost territories in the American Southwest. The movement used the ancient Aztec word *Aztlán* to refer to California, Nevada, Arizona, Utah, New Mexico, and Colorado, which were ceded to the United States in 1848. The theory holds that by infiltrating the border with overwhelming numbers of migrants, if not arms, the lost lands of Aztlán would eventually revert to Mexico.

I became aware of the Aztlán movement when I covered the Tierra Amarilla Land Grant protest in the late 1980s. At the time, I paid little attention to it, considering it to be more rhetoric than reality. As the

SPLC points out, the origins of the conspiracy theory can be traced to the *Plan Espiritual de Aztlán*, a document reportedly adopted in 1969 at the First National Chicano Liberation Youth Conference that originated with the student group MEChA, or Movimiento Estudiantil Chicano de Aztlán. Although the document did little more than reflect the resurgence of ethnic pride at the time, the SPLC notes that Spencer and his fellow anti-immigration activists such as the late Barbara Coe, who headed a group called the California Coalition for Immigration Reform, used it as proof that all Mexican Americans wanted to reconquer the American Southwest and return it to Mexico.

As Southern California became increasingly Latino, losing its white majority, and the provisions of Proposition 187 were met by an immediate court challenge, Spencer left California for Arizona, with the intention, he tells me, to focus on the unfinished task of securing the whole of the US border. Days after the proposition passed in November 1994, a federal district court judge ruled that it violated the US Constitution and issued an injunction blocking it. In July 1999 parties on both sides of the issue signed an agreement that effectively gutted the proposition and affirmed that key provisions were unconstitutional.

Spencer's move to Arizona was also prompted by Operation Gatekeeper, which had tightened the border in San Diego to the west and in El Paso to the east, forcing illegal immigration into more rural areas along the border in southern Arizona. In 2002, the SPLC notes, Spencer aligned with other anti-immigrant activists broadly known as "minutemen," some of whom had also apparently relocated from elsewhere to the southern Arizona border, which had become the focus of illegal immigration activity.

While Spencer sees himself as a warrior fighting a rising tide of illegality, the SPLC takes a dim view of the man, calling him "a vitriolic Mexican-basher and self-appointed guardian of the border who may have done more than anyone to spread the myth of a secret Mexican conspiracy to reconquer the Southwest."

Spencer is kept company on his borderland *ranchito* by seven German shepherds that he treats as family and who have the run of the house. When I ask Spencer about his portrayal by the SPLC, he shrugs it off as a hazard of the business. The idea is to "demonize the opposition," he says, rather than argue the veracity of his claims.

"I'm labeled a hate group. That is why the media won't talk to me. That's how they shut me up. What they bring up [about me] is absolutely vacuous." Spencer notes that he has been a successful businessman: "I used to run a seismic oil company." Now, his American Border Patrol has been mischaracterized as a "militia," he says, which it is not and has never been. "We were not part of the minutemen groups, ever," he says—but the link did give the American Border Patrol some recognition. "I think it was worth it to call attention to the [border] problem."

His group is only interested in activism. "We're trying to spark action. We're not a hate group." By using his small drone and his ultralight, Spencer says, he goaded the government into doing something along the Arizona border. "They would never have done anything if we had not said anything." This is why Spencer came to Arizona. "The only time the government does anything is when they're shamed into doing it."

Some think Spencer went too far, however, when he simulated the smuggling of a nuclear weapon into the United States by driving a truck across the border from Mexico carrying a supposed bomb-in-a-box while filming the entire escapade. Spencer drove what he describes as "a smugglers' truck" up the dry streambed of the San Pedro River (one of only two rivers that flow northward from Mexico into the United States) and then into Tucson, where he parked it in front of the federal building. He gave the video to local television stations, but he remains angry that his project did not attract any national media attention. "Did anybody come? No. We never got any national coverage on it."

For many years the US Border Patrol's radio transmissions were not encrypted and could be monitored. So when Spencer overheard that the Border Patrol was chasing a group of illegal immigrants, he would take to the air and track the event. He was then accused of chasing immigrants himself, he says, but denies that ever happened. "I've

never chased anybody," he says. "It's pure BS. We do patrol the border, but it is high tech." In reality, he confides, "we patrol the Border
Patrol." In 2006 he made video recordings of the Border Patrol's bum-
bling efforts to find suspected illegal migrants, and only after he made
the radio transmissions public, "[the Border Patrol] started scram-
bling their radio [traffic]."

His Border Patrol–tracking activities can be followed at the group's
website, he says, under the title of Operation B.E.E.F., an acronym for
Border Enforcement Evaluation First. One of the group's main tasks
is to track the progress of the construction of seven hundred miles of
fence along the US-Mexico border, which was called for in the Secure
Fence Act of 2006. A year after the act became law, only two miles of
fence had been built, he says. The following year, what was called a
"virtual fence" was being built, consisting of a series of high-tech surveillance towers, which he calls a billion-dollar disaster.

The virtual fence was formally known as the Secure Border Initiative network, or SBInet, and was built by the Boeing Company, the
passenger jet manufacturer based in Seattle, Washington, under a
three-year contract with the Department of Homeland Security estimated at about $10 billion. The concept was to build a system of sur-
veillance towers along the six thousand miles of both the Mexican and
Canadian borders, and link them with a central command. The initial
phase of the contract was called Project 28, and for about $67 million,
Boeing was going to cover just twenty-eight miles along the border
near Nogales, Arizona, with the virtual fence.

Problems quickly surfaced. Although the towers went up in June
2007, the Border Patrol complained that they weren't connected
properly. In effect, the system didn't work, and the virtual fence was
lambasted by borderland residents and human rights activists. In the
town of Arivaca, just ten miles north of the border, residents said the
government was spying on them rather than hunting for migrants.
They feared being profiled and subjected to false arrest and imprison-
ment if they happened to be Hispanic. Activists feared they would be
arrested by the Border Patrol as they wandered the area to replenish
their humanitarian water drops.

berto, a migrant from Guatemala, found wandering the southern Arizona desert.

Ed McCullough, left, inspects a water jug with Al Enciso, near the US-Mexico border.

Discarded migrant backpack in the southern Arizona desert.

McCullough looks at a map of migrant trails in southern Arizona.

ther Peter Neeley, center, with migrants and deportees at El Comedor, Nogales, Sonora.

Migrants and deportees eating breakfast at El Comedor dining hall in Nogales, Sonora.

Adelaydo Cornejo Hernandez, a deportee from California, at El Comedor, holds a photo of his daughter, a US citizen.

grants get medicine at a free clinic in Nogales, Sonora.

uth American sheepherders in western Colorado.

Juan Chumacero Sr. helps sheepherders in Rangely, Colorado.

istobal, a former drug addict, at a drug rehabilitation center in Agua Prieta, Sonora.

cole Lawson, mayor of Columbus, New Mexico.

Phillip Skinner at his restaurant's kitchen in Columbus, New Mexico.

Sergio and Ivonne Romero, Palomas, Chihuahua.

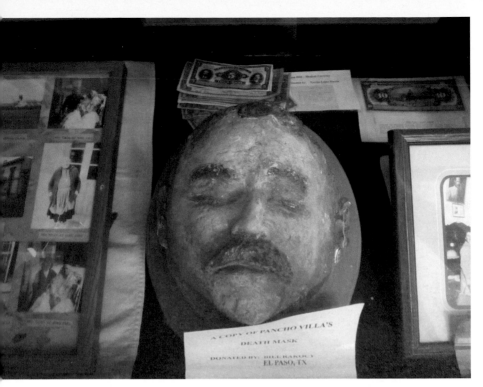

py of Pancho Villa's death mask, Columbus Historical Museum, Columbus, New Mexico.

Richard Dean of Columbus, New Mexico, whose great-grandfather died in Pancho Villa's 1916 raid.

Glenn Spencer at the truncated border fence on his ranch in southern Arizona.

Author with pepper-spray gun and Border Patrol agent George Schmid.

rder Patrol agent Brent Cagen holding rocks typically thrown at agents and vehicles.

ny Estrada, sheriff of Santa Cruz County, Arizona, a critic of Arizona immigration laws.

Virtual border fence tower, west of Nogales, Arizona, on the US-Mexico border.

Captured migrants wearing camouflaged clothing and carpet booties in Buenos Aires National Wild
Refuge, near Sasabe, Arizona.

fiscated migrant backpacks at a Border Patrol processing center, Tucson, Arizona.

mmy Bassett, right, with Daniel Cifuentes in the Just Coffee roasting house in Agua Prieta, Sonora.

David and Lilia Cifuentes in Salvador Urbina, Chiapas.

Guatemalan coffee picker with grower Isaac Cifuentes, right, in Salvador Urbina, Chiapas.

Ripe coffee beans in Salvador Urbina, Chiapas.

Roblero Mendez washing coffee beans at his home in El Aguila, Chiapas.

The church at Salvador Urbina.

National heroes Emiliano Zapata, left, and Pancho Villa in lights on the Zócalo plaza in Mexico City, Mexico.

After the initial twenty-eight miles of virtual fence went online in early 2008, the project was extended by another twenty-five miles. In January 2011, however, with the cost of the project skyrocketing under repeated overruns and delays, Homeland Security secretary Janet Napolitano canceled the Boeing contract. For a total price tag of nearly $1 billion, a total of fifty-three miles had been covered. Napolitano said the department was going to go back to readily available, off-the-shelf technology for border enforcement.

Spencer says the virtual fence debacle is an example of the government's phony efforts to secure the border. "It was never intended to work," he says. The virtual fence was put in some places where physical fences already existed, he says. "It was all about putting on a show," Spencer suggests, and the purpose was to get Congress to approve an amnesty for the estimated twelve million undocumented immigrants already in the country. "They killed [the virtual fence] because they didn't get amnesty."

Spencer suspects that the estimated twelve million illegal migrants now in the country may actually number about fifty million, if one includes their families, and argues that no one knows the real number. Talk of amnesty only encourages more migration from Mexico, Spencer says. "If we have another amnesty, the Southwest will belong to Mexico. I am sure of it."

I ask Spencer why he insists that the government does not want to secure the border when hundreds of miles of an impenetrable fence have been built. Meanwhile, the Border Patrol has more than doubled in size and billions of dollars are spent each year on enforcement.

He answers that the government is "infiltrated by left-wing, open-border people. They want open borders. They are leftists, if not communists."

"Why would leftists want open borders?" I ask.

Open-border proponents believe that "if capital crosses borders, why can't people?" he says. But the porous border is ruining the American economy. "We are importing poverty on a mass scale."

Spencer says that because of the "essentially open border" along Southern California, the Californian culture is actually "a Mexican culture." As the influx of Mexicans continues, Spencer fears that once Mexicans obtain a popular majority, "they may vote to leave the union." To illustrate his point, Spencer shows me a video from 1987 when former Mexican president Ernesto Zedillo addressed the National Council of La Raza in Los Angeles and told the group that the nation of Mexico extends beyond the border and includes all Mexican immigrants in the United States, legal or otherwise.

Since Mexico allows dual citizenship, Spencer says, Mexicans can vote in the United States "in the interests of Mexico. There is a subversive movement in our country engineered by the Mexican government. It is aided and abetted by Obama" and his immigration policies. "[Obama] hasn't done any [security] on the border. It was all done under Bush." Spencer says of Mexicans, "They're coming across the border to take their land back. That's why they have a lot of babies. They don't assimilate. They swim in their own ocean."

Our conversation is tinged with paranoia as Spencer explains that he became a target when he openly criticized former Los Angeles mayor Antonio Villaraigosa in a full-page advertisement he bought in the *Los Angeles Daily News* that read, "Does Los Angeles Need a Mayor Who Reports to Mexico City?" Villaraigosa resisted Proposition 187, Spencer says.

Throughout his anti-immigration battles, including Proposition 187, Spencer says his attorneys have been harassed and intimidated. One attorney's house was broken into and swastikas were painted on the house. Clothes were put on a bed, a symbol of impending death. One attorney disappeared, he says. "I have seen such power behind the movement to open the border with Mexico that it is frightening." The proponents will "destroy anyone who is resisting this movement. I am enemy number one by the open-border community. They want to shut me up. They came after me because I know too much. I can document it."

I tell Spencer that should not be surprising since he has been tied to some of the most extreme elements of the border vigilante movement. Perhaps the most problematic are his past brushes with Shawna

Forde, a forty-three-year-old former beautician and border vigilante who was convicted of masterminding a May 2009 home invasion that left a nine-year-old girl, Brisenia Flores, and her father, Raul Flores, dead in their home in Arivaca, Arizona. Two years later, on February 22, 2011, Forde was sentenced to death for her role in the killings. As of this writing, she sits on Arizona's death row while her conviction is on appeal.

According to a February 2011 report on the killings in the online *Daily Beast*, Forde and two accomplices entered the Flores mobile home wearing camouflaged clothing and with blackened faces, apparently posing as police officers searching for fugitives. In reality, the three reportedly were looking for money and drugs, which testimony revealed Forde had said she wanted to take from area drug dealers to support her small vigilante group called the Minutemen American Defense. When neither were found, and Raul Flores questioned whether the three were really police, he was shot. Moments later Flores's wife, Gina Gonzalez, was also shot and wounded. She played dead, apparently hoping the three would leave. Instead, one of the men shot Flores five more times, then reloaded his pistol and shot nine-year-old Brisenia twice in the head as the child pleaded for her life.

Forde's accomplices were Jason Eugene "Gunny" Bush, a white supremacist from the Pacific Northwest, who had a prison record and was said to be the trigger man, and Albert Gaxiola, a resident of Arivaca, who reportedly wanted Flores killed because he was competition in the area's drug trade. Following his trial, Bush was sentenced to death by lethal injection in early April 2011 for the murders of Flores and his daughter. At the time of his sentencing, Bush faced two additional murder charges in Washington State. One was in connection with a July 1997 fatal stabbing of a man in Wenatchee. A second was in connection with the shooting death in September 1997 of a man near Palisades. As of this writing, Bush is on death row in Arizona while appeals are considered. Gaxiola was also convicted in the murder case in July 2011 and sentenced to life in prison without parole.

Forde and Bush had troubled histories. According to reports, Forde was the seventh of nine children, five from different fathers, and was the victim of intergenerational sexual and physical abuse, according to her defense attorneys. She was put in foster care and adopted at the age of five, and lived in several homes where she continued to be molested and abused.

According to defense witnesses, Forde shoplifted as a teenager, ran away from home, and survived on the streets of Seattle as a prostitute. She reportedly attempted suicide three times by drug overdoses, was married and divorced five times, and gave birth to three children, one of whom apparently died of sudden infant death syndrome in Alaska. According to testimony at her trial, Forde was described as emotionally detached, possessed below-average intelligence, and suffered from personality disorders, impaired insight, and lack of judgment. Forde never apologized during the trial, which her attorney explained was due to the fact that she was mentally ill.

Bush was equally troubled. Attorneys said Bush was difficult from the age of two and his parents disowned him at the age of eleven, committing him to a mental institution where he was reportedly sexually abused. Bush was then in and out of jail and prison, where attorneys said he never received proper help and guidance.

Spencer says his contact with Forde was minimal. At one point, Forde asked Spencer if she could use the motor home he had on his property, hoping her sixteen-year-old daughter could stay there. "I put the word out that she was not welcome here," Spencer says. The morning of the murder of Flores and his daughter, however, Forde visited Spencer and used the Internet, he says, then left. The day that Forde was arrested, FBI agents came to his house, but Spencer was never charged in the case.

Despite his controversial reputation, Spencer believes he has had a profound impact on the border and points to the fact that the drug cartels are fighting one another over control of drug smuggling corridors into the United States. "Fighting over corridors?" Spencer asks rhetorically. Smuggling corridors would not exist if it were not for the border fences—the same fences that Spencer says he and others have demanded for more than twenty years, which have forced drug smugglers and human traffickers into the remote areas now termed corridors.

An example, Spencer says, is the Barry Goldwater bombing range on the border in southwestern Arizona below Yuma. "This is a bombing range and there was no fence," Spencer says. "It was a huge corridor, perfect for smuggling drugs," and was crisscrossed with the tire tracks of dune buggies hauling tons of drugs into the United States. When it was finally fenced, drug smugglers "had to go somewhere else, and that [elsewhere] belonged to someone else. Before the fence, [cartels] weren't fighting over corridors."

Spencer admits that he has considered giving up. "Ten years ago I was going to shut it all down," but confesses that, "I couldn't leave this thing," which is why he moved to Arizona and settled on the border. "A good general picks his battles. I wanted to fight this battle on the border," he says, where "it's a lot easier to expose [the government]. We've done that. It's what I came here to do."

## The Man Behind Senate Bill 1070

One the most controversial laws of recent years has been Arizona's Senate Bill 1070, widely known as the show-me-your-papers law. According to an official summary of the bill, the law "requires a reasonable attempt to be made to determine the immigration status of a person during any legitimate contact made by an official or agency of the state or a county, city, town or political subdivision *if reasonable suspicion exists* [italic added] that the person is an alien who is unlawfully present in the US."

Soon after Governor Jan Brewer signed the bill into law on April 23, 2010, it was challenged by the United States Department of Justice, which contended that the bill usurped the authority of federal government to control and enforce immigration. A federal judge issued a preliminary injunction that blocked the law while it was appealed.

Two years later in June 2012, the US Supreme Court ruled that checking of the immigration status of a person during a local law enforcement stop was legal, but the court rejected three other parts of the law. The court ruled that Arizona can't charge immigrants with a misdemeanor if they're not carrying proper immigration documents, can't charge illegal immigrants with a crime for seeking work, and can't let law officers arrest someone solely on the suspicion that he or she may have committed a crime for which he or she could be deported.

In late October 2012 I meet with the sponsor of Senate Bill 1070, former Arizona senator Russell Pearce, in his favorite café in Mesa, a suburb of Phoenix. When I explain to the waitress who I am meeting, she shows me to the café's John Wayne room, saying that is where Pearce has all of his meetings. Senate Bill 1070 was not Pearce's only bill on immigration. He has been involved in a range of earlier similar issues, such as a law to prove citizenship prior to voting, a law to prevent illegal immigrants from being released from jail on bond, and an English-only law.

Pearce is proud that he is a fifth-generation Arizonan. According to his website biography, he had a tough childhood and was one of thirteen children in a blended family. He worked as a deputy in the Maricopa County Sheriff's Office from 1970 until 1991, and will never forget an encounter with several Hispanics that left him wounded. On July 1977 while on patrol, Pearce spotted three teenagers drinking beer. When he confronted them, one of the young men ordered his Doberman to attack Pearce. While struggling with the dog, Pearce's gun was taken. Pearce fought off the dog, and as he tried to retrieve his gun, one of the teenagers shot him. The bullet took off the ring finger of his right hand and slammed into his chest. Though wounded, Pearce was able to force one of the teens into his squad car, and after calling for backup, chased the others. He received a medal for his efforts.

After working as justice of the peace for more than a year, Pearce returned to the Maricopa County Sheriff's Office as the chief deputy in 1993 for Sheriff Joe Arpaio. Among other things, Pearce helped create the county's infamous tent-city jail, a low-cost incarceration center that prevented the county from having to build a multimillion-dollar permanent structure. In 1995 Pearce was named director of the Arizona Motor Vehicle Department, and in 2000 he was elected to the Arizona Senate. After a decade of pushing conservative causes, most notably SB 1070, he was defeated in a November 2011 recall election. In August 2012 Pearce lost a comeback bid in the Republican primary for a state senate seat.

Among some of Pearce's most criticized associations has been with Jason Todd "JT" Ready, whom the Southern Poverty Law Center describes as "a former member of the neo-Nazi National Socialist Movement (NSM), specialized in bashing immigrants." According to the center's profile on Ready, the former US Marine was court-martialed twice and discharged from the marines for bad conduct in 1996. Ready returned to Arizona, where he ran for various Arizona offices, including the Mesa City Council and the Arizona Legislature, failing in both. In June 2010, according to the SPLC, "Ready led a group of armed extremists—called the U.S. Border Guard—into the Arizona desert to apprehend immigrants and drug smugglers."

The group reportedly included Jeff Hall, of Riverside, California, who was a rabid member of the NSM, the nation's largest neo-Nazi group. In May 2011 Hall was reportedly shot and killed by his ten-year-old son as Hall slept on the couch in his living room.

Ready died an equally violent death. In May 2012 the thirty-nine-year-old apparently shot and killed his girlfriend and three others, including a toddler, at a house in Gilbert, Arizona, then turned his gun on himself. Authorities said the cause was domestic violence issues. At the time of his death, Ready was reportedly being investigated by the FBI for domestic terrorism.

Pearce bristles at the reports that connect him with Ready and insists that he hardly knew the man. On his website, Pearce writes this about Ready: "When we first met JT, he was fresh out of the Marine Corps and seemed like a decent person." But "at some point in time darkness took his life over, his heart changed, and he began to associate with the more despicable groups in society. They were intolerant and hateful and like so many who knew him from before, I was upset and disappointed at the choices he was making. I worked with others to have him removed from his local position within our Republican Party because there has never been and will never be any room in our party or our lives for those preaching hatred."

When Pearce arrives at the café and I explain that I want to talk about border issues and immigrants, Pearce immediately offers, "If the government wanted the border secured, we would have done it long ago."

"Who opposes a secure border?" I ask.

Two groups, he says. One wants to change the demographics of the country and alter voting constituencies. The second group is business owners who hire undocumented workers and place "profits over patriotism." More people should share his concerns about the border, Pearce says. "It's disappointing that we have people who stand on the sidelines and do not help secure this country." Illegal immigration is subversive, Pearce says, and claims that nine thousand people per year die at the hands of "illegal aliens."

When I question the number, he asks, "If it's only half of that, is it OK?"

Accurate numbers on crimes committed by migrants in Arizona or the United States illegally are difficult to find. According to a report produced by www.cityrating.com, the crime rate in Arizona for 2013 was expected to be lower than in 2010, when the state violent crime rate was higher than the national violent crime average by 31.73 percent. The site, which relies on current FBI crime statistics, also reported that the Arizona property crime rate was higher than the national property crime rate average by 80.08 percent. Regarding murders, a 2008 study by researchers at Johns Hopkins University about firearm homicides, published in the *Journal of Urban Health*, revealed that urban young blacks between the ages of twenty-five and forty-four were the most likely to die gun-related deaths, followed by young white males of similar age. The overall homicide rate of about six per one hundred thousand population was pretty much uniform across the United States, and Arizona was not among the states noted in the study with the worst problem. Given that the worst murder rate was among black males, and demographically blacks are not a significant portion of the Arizona population, Pearce's death rate claims are dubious.

But crime is only one concern. The flood of undocumented workers in the country is creating "artificially low wages," he says, which suppress the national economy. In addition, the presence of some twelve million undocumented people in the United States is expensive. "The result of the burden of the illegal alien invasion is $113 billion a year," he says, a figure that is espoused by the Federation for American Immigration Reform (FAIR), an anti-immigrant lobbying group based in Washington, DC. That estimated figure is the cost of educating, providing medical care, and incarcerating people who are in the country illegally, he says. "The American people pay a price for this," which is why he has supported a host of measures that prevent those who are in the United States illegally from either receiving benefits or from staying. "There's nothing that says you can't call [Immigration and Customs Enforcement] when you have someone who [has circumvented] the system."

Those who oppose these measures "support lawbreakers over law keepers," Pearce says. Why should people be able to enter the United States and help themselves to jobs, public schools, health care, and public assistance? he asks. "You can't walk into my house and help yourself to my refrigerator."

When I note that most people who cross the border illegally come because they can find work, Pearce says he supports sanctions against businesses that hire undocumented workers. "If you knowingly hire an illegal alien," it should lead to revocation of a business license, he says.

His controversial Senate Bill 1070 "grew out of sanctuary policies," Pearce says, promoted by those who believe that people who are in the United States illegally should be helped, not hindered. SB 1070 allows local law officers to cooperate with federal ICE officials to find and deport people who shouldn't be in the United States. "We don't need immigration reform, we need immigration enforcement."

"You and others have been accused of racism and advocating the rounding up of suspected undocumented workers," I say.

"You don't need roundups," he says with a shake of his head. The illegal population can be reduced through "attrition by enforcement." People crossing the border illegally will be much less willing to do so if they know there are no benefits to be collected and that they can be arrested, he says. "You'll go somewhere else."

Pearce disputes the contention of the US Justice Department that only the federal government has the power to enforce immigration law. "States have the inherent authority to enforce immigration law," he says. "There has never been a preemptive policy to stop a state from enforcing immigration law. I don't need a stinking permission slip from the federal government to enforce the law. If they don't do their job, it's malfeasance. Shame on them."

Pearce began working on what became SB 1070 back in 2005. At that time, an event occurred in his personal life that shook him deeply and may have cemented his convictions about the law and immigration. On December 16, 2004, according to a report in the *Arizona Republic* newspaper, Pearce's son, Sean, an eleven-year veteran of the Maricopa County Sheriff's Office, was shot while serving an arrest warrant at a Mesa mobile home. The shooter was a twenty-two-year-old undocumented migrant who hid behind a Christmas tree and fired a gun when Sean Pearce entered the home.

Pearce says he was delivering a speech in Washington, DC, when he received the news of his son's shooting. In 2005 he told the *Arizona Republic* that the shooting "must be kept in perspective," and that "I've tried avoid being unfair about this whole thing," even as he continued to sponsor a range of immigration enforcement bills. Pearce insists that his and his son's shootings have not colored his opinions of Mexicans. "I don't hate the men who shot me or my son, but I know my duty. What I'm mad at is my government. [The shootings] should not have happened."

Pearce says he is motivated, too, by the many Arizonans he's met and known who also have been victims of attacks by undocumented migrants. Perhaps the most important was the March 2010 shooting death of Arizona rancher Robert Krentz Jr., fifty-eight, from one of the state's prominent ranching families. On the day of his death, Krentz was riding his all-terrain vehicle on a remote corner of this ranch near the border, which had been the scene in the past of drug and illegal immigration trafficking. Krentz radioed to his brother that he had stopped and was helping someone who he thought was a migrant, then went missing after the call. His body was found several hours later, still in his all-terrain vehicle. Krentz had been shot to death. Investigators followed footprints to the border and assumed the tracks were those of the shooter.

Krentz's death came just as the Arizona legislature was considering SB 1070, and the public outrage at the killing spurred its passage. "Krentz was a friend of mine," Pearce says, and the killing affected him deeply. After Krentz was killed, ranchers along the border called to tell him that their guard dogs were being killed, their fences were being torn down, and their water tanks were being destroyed. Ranchers told him, "We pray for daylight because we don't dare go out at night," Pearce says. "It makes you realize how dangerous the border is" because of the "illegal alien invasion."

While remote border ranch land is favored by smugglers of people and drugs, available crime statistics show that Arizona border towns such as Nogales appear to be safer than many other cities in the state. This could be attributed to the massive presence of border security personnel, because Nogales is a major port of entry. According to www.cityrating.com, the violent crime rate for Nogales in 2010 was one-third lower than the national rate, but the property crime rate in Nogales was one-third higher than the national rate. In comparison with the rest of Arizona, the 2010 violent crime rate in Nogales was also more than one-third lower than the state's rate, but the property crime rate in Nogales was about 10 percent higher than the state rate.

Yuma, however, was more crime-ridden that the rest of Arizona, according to the website. In 2010 the violent crime rate in Yuma was more than 50 percent higher than the rest of Arizona, but the property crime rate in Yuma was slightly lower than the statewide rate. The Yuma violent crime rate for 2010 was higher than the national rate by more than 50 percent, and the property crime rate was 17 percent higher than the national rate.

## The Kobach Effect

As the bill that eventually became SB 1070 began to take shape, Pearce confirms, he contacted Kris Kobach, the conservative attorney who became the Kansas secretary of state. A former law professor with a law degree from Yale and a graduate of Harvard and Oxford, Kobach is a self-described "litigator who fights for the rights of U.S. citizens in cases involving illegal immigration." Kobach was a top counsel to conservative former US attorney general John Ashcroft and a former chairman of the Kansas Republican Party. "I contacted Kris Kobach," Pearce says, calling him the country's top authority on states' rights, and "a very good friend of mine. I solicited his help in 2010" as SB 1070 was being finalized.

Pearce says he also worked with FAIR, which describes itself as a "national, nonprofit, public-interest, membership organization of concerned citizens who share a common belief that our nation's immigration policies must be reformed to serve the national interest." According to the FAIR website, the group has 250,000 members and "seeks to improve border security, to stop illegal immigration, and to promote immigration levels consistent with the national interest—more traditional rates of about 300,000 a year."

The Southern Poverty Law Center does not share Pearce's admiration for either Kobach or FAIR. The SPLC lists Kobach as a "nativist" and describes him as "the man behind many of the deeply flawed anti-illegal immigrant laws passed recently." Kobach formerly worked for the Immigration Reform Law Institute, which the SPLC says is the legal arm of FAIR, which the center also lists as a nativist, anti-immigration group. "Although FAIR maintains a veneer of legitimacy that has allowed its principals to testify in Congress and lobby the federal government, this veneer hides much ugliness," the SPLC says on its website. "FAIR leaders have ties to white supremacist groups and eugenicists [advocates of selective human breeding] and have made many racist statements."

Pearce chafes at the suggestion that he didn't write the bill and that Kobach and other corporate interests, such as private prison companies, did the drafting. "I wrote the bill," he tells me, "but we were going to get sued. We wanted it to be sued. We were begging for a Supreme Court battle. You know the games you have to have with the black robes." Pearce consulted Kobach so that language in the bill could withstand a legal challenge, he explains.

Laws such as SB 1070 and other similar laws that have surfaced in Alabama, Georgia, Pennsylvania, and Texas are of interest to companies such as the Corrections Corporation of America (CCC), which contract with state and federal agencies to incarcerate inmates and illegal immigrants.

An investigative report produced in October 2010 by National Public Radio stated that Arizona's SB 1070 was reviewed at a meeting of the American Legislative Exchange Council (ALEC). According to the ALEC website, the group is a "forum for state legislators and private sector leaders to discuss and exchange practical, state-level public policy issues." In reality, the group is a place where the country's largest corporations, the prime sponsors of ALEC, meet with lobbyists and state legislators from around the country to discuss and promote laws that benefit corporate and socially conservative ideas. Pearce told NPR that he attended an ALEC meeting in December 2009 in Washington, DC, and made a presentation to about fifty people, including officials from the CCC. "I went through the facts. I went through the impacts, and they said, 'Yeah,'" Pearce told NPR. SB 1070 was clearly of interest to CCC because, according to the NPR report, "executives believe immigrant detention is their next big market."

ALEC, meanwhile, admits that it develops "model" legislation. "Unlike in many private sector groups that offer model legislation, elected state legislators fully control ALEC's model legislation process," the group's website states. Once the organization vets a draft bill, it is then "posted for other ALEC members" to use or not use.

Alabama is one of the states that adopted an immigration bill similar to Arizona's SB 1070. In an October 2011 blog written by journalist George Talbot for the *Press-Register* of Mobile, Alabama, Kobach said he was happy to have been behind the bill. "I'm proud to have been part of it, and the untold story is how successful it has already been in opening jobs for Alabama citizens," Kobach said, suggesting that undocumented workers were taking jobs from state residents.

Ironically, even as Kobach was bragging about the bill, groups of Alabama farmers were up in arms because their crops went unpicked and were rotting in their fields. Alabama residents were unwilling to pick them, and the Mexican migrants who normally did the work had been scared off by the law. The farmers feared they would lose their farms if they couldn't pick and sell their produce.

The same thing was happening in October 2011 in the neighboring state of Georgia, where a similar migrant worker crackdown had been signed into law. In an October 2011 story by the Associated Press, Charles Hall of the Georgia Fruit and Vegetables Growers Association said that Georgia farmers had lost $75 million that year because of unpicked crops. The Georgia farmers said they had lost 40 percent of their workforce thanks to the immigrant crackdown.

But the effects didn't end after one harvest. Six months later, in the spring of 2012, Alabama farmers were still reeling from the effects of the law and were planting less, hoping to avoid another year of crippling losses caused by unpicked crops. Tomato farmer Keith Dickie told an Associated Press reporter in May 2012 that he didn't plant part of his forty acres because he feared the tomatoes would never be picked. Planting less still might not solve the labor shortage, he complained. If he lost money for a second year, he said, "I guess we'll sell out and find something else to do."

The agricultural crisis caused by the immigration crackdown did not concern Kobach, who crowed, "There haven't been mass arrests. There aren't a bunch of court proceedings. People are simply removing themselves. It's self-deportation at no cost to the taxpayer. I'd say that's a win."

Despite the controversy around SB 1070, Pearce says the results of the law in Arizona are good. "Crime has dropped to three times below the national average," and crime in Phoenix is at a thirty-year low. "We have a declining jail and prison population." It is due to his law, he says; "There is no other explanation for it." Recent crime data, however, as referenced earlier, show that such a precipitous drop has not happened and cannot be attributed to the law.

But the controversy around SB 1070 ultimately pushed him out of office, I say.

Pearce shakes his head at the thought. "We suspect a lot of voter fraud" occurred in the recall election. "Were they misled and deceived?" he asks of voters. "Absolutely. Was it disappointing? Yes." Pearce says he has no plans to quit, however. "I've been in this battle for twenty-five years. I don't have any plans to retreat."

## America's Toughest Sheriff

One of the most vocal, visible, and controversial figures in the immigration debate is Arizona's Maricopa County sheriff Joe Arpaio. When I meet with Arpaio, often called "America's toughest sheriff," at his office on the upper floors of a high-rise building in downtown Phoenix in mid-November 2012, he has just been reelected to his sixth four-year term. It was an election that cost $8.5 million, a political war chest that delivered for him an overwhelming majority of the votes. Arpaio regularly appears on national television, where he offers acerbic assessments of the state of immigration, border security, and immigration enforcement. There is never any doubt that he comes down on the side of strict law and order.

Among the building blocks of the Arpaio legend is his tent-city jail, where inmates are clad in pink overalls. An army veteran and former policeman in Washington, DC, and Las Vegas, he also worked as a federal narcotics agent in Turkey, the Middle East, Mexico, and Central and South America, ultimately landing in the US Drug Enforcement Administration. He was first sworn in as sheriff of Maricopa County in 1993.

Arpaio bristles at the mention of the lawsuits against him and his department, especially one by the federal Justice Department for "discriminatory and otherwise unconstitutional law enforcement actions against Latinos." The lawsuits are politically motivated, he says. "It all has to do with votes. It's sad. It should have to do with what is right."

"We don't racially profile," Arpaio says. "It's a lot of propaganda. Profiling? It's not happening. It was misunderstood." His department does not depend on federal law, because local and state laws are sufficient for him to do his job. "We charge everyone under state charges in lieu of turning them over to the federal Immigration and Customs Enforcement agency."

"Why do you focus on immigrants and not the people who employ them?" I ask.

"We have the e-Verify program for those employers who unknowingly hire" undocumented migrants, Arpaio says. But "most [migrants] have fake identification," he says. By arresting such people, "we go in there to reduce the identity-theft problem."

Arpaio is sensitive about his reputation. "I'm the bad guy," he says with resignation, but adds that, "law enforcement does have a say in reducing illegal immigration."

While many people argue that the reduced number of illegal border crossings is due to the bad economy, Arpaio disagrees. "You can't prove it by me. The economy has gone down, [but] I don't see a reduction in illegal aliens coming into our country."

Hispanics had a strong hand in the reelection of President Obama and returning more Democrats to Congress, I note. "Does that make you think more about catering to the Hispanic community, as some ranking Republicans have done?" I ask.

Arpaio shrugs. "I don't worry about that; a lot of Hispanics did oppose me. I still won. The Republican Party is revisiting this problem. They're afraid [Hispanics] will gang up on them." Arpaio admits, however, that the 2012 election was "a wake-up call" and may push Congress to "make laws more conducive to the Mexican American community. Politicians want to get reelected."

Arpaio's reelection cost $8.5 million. "That's an extremely high amount for a county sheriff election," I say.

"I needed it," Arpaio replies. "I had everyone zero in on me. They thought they had me this time. I'm the only one standing."

Even so, Arpaio intends an image makeover. "When I got reelected, I said I'm going to reach out in a civil way. I've got to find a way to change [critics'] minds to explain why I do these things. But I'm still going to do my job, which is to enforce the laws." Arpaio says he is more in touch with minority communities than most people realize. "I do reach out. I feel very comfortable with the black and Hispanic neighborhoods more than with the higher-class communities."

His potential outreach includes the White House. "I'd like to get the president to visit me, too. I'd like to have a beer with him. We'd have some fun together." Immigration is not a partisan issue, he says. "It's everybody's problem."

But Arpaio's idea of fun is undoubtedly different from President Obama's. Arpaio used his office to launch his own investigation into the legitimacy of Obama's Hawaiian birth certificate, part of the Birthers movement. "I believe the government documents [provided by Obama] are a fraud," he says. "If that birth certificate is a phony, it means the president wasn't born here."

"Why is Obama's birth certificate of interest to the department?" I ask.

"What concerns America also concerns the people of Maricopa County," Arpaio says.

"What did you find?"

"Anyone who pays a water bill can get a birth certificate in Hawaii," he says. "I thought that would be a big story," but no national media picked it up. Arpaio's investigators also tracked down the ninety-year-old woman who actually signed Obama's certificate.

"What did she say?"

"She doesn't remember signing it," Arpaio says with a shake of his head. She signed many thousands of birth certificates in her career. "Why doesn't Congress look into this?" Arpaio asks, noting that Obama's Selective Service card is questionable because it lacks an official stamp. "Why is his different?"

Arpaio admits that he has been very public in his anti–illegal immigration campaign. "I've been very visible. When I have raids, I'm out there loading them [into vehicles]. I became very vocal and visible. I did it on purpose." But such visibility has its downsides, he says, since his comments generate sympathy for mistreated migrants. "There's a movement to use me as the poster boy to get amnesty. I am against amnesty. It's not right to reward people who came in illegally."

Because of his experience working with the DEA in foreign countries, Arpaio is convinced that more can and should be done to battle the drug cartels and staunch the flow of narcotics into the United States. It simply requires "boots on the ground" in Mexico and Guatemala, he says, and for the president to say, "We're going to stop this on the Mexican side of the border."

When I remark that such an aggressive approach would be dangerous, Arpaio says, "So? Send in the army. We have a neighbor called Mexico and we're not trying to help them. With mutual trust, we can do it. The history is there, if you can get through the public relations and the government."

Arpaio recalls with a smile the dawn of the war on drugs, when President Richard Nixon, angry that Mexico refused to cooperate on their side of the border with his freshly declared war, closed all ports of entry and ordered each car from Mexico to be thoroughly inspected before it could enter the United States. "We stopped every car crossing the border. We were willing to back them up all the way to Mexico City."

The move forced Mexico to work with US antinarcotics agents. The same could be done to stem the flow of illegal immigration, Arpaio says. "Let's talk about the whole problem. Why isn't the Mexican government cracking down on illegal immigration?" he asks. Then he offers, "Mexico wants them to come," because "the money from here [earned by migrants] is going back to Mexico. It's a big income for them."

When Mexico is criticized for its lack of assistance in curbing illegal immigration, "they play the race card," he says, claiming that critics of their lack of cooperation are anti-Mexican. Meanwhile, US business owners stay silent because "they like to have the cheap labor."

Despite his age—Arpaio turned eighty years old in 2012—the sheriff is undeterred. "What's eighty?" he asks. "I'm going to keep doing it and not back down. They took all their shots. It's the first time I've seen so much against me." He pauses and smiles, clearly relishing the fight. "This election was the most satisfying for me," and he looks to the future, planning to run for sheriff again in 2016 for an unprecedented seventh term.

## The Case Against SB 1070

Although Arpaio has broad support, a national reputation, and a seemingly impregnable political machine, some in Phoenix object to the sheriff's tactics. Among them is Alessandra Soler, executive director of the American Civil Liberties Union of Arizona. On a warm and sunny day in October 2012, I meet with her in the ACLU's Phoenix office. Living in the midst of anti-immigrant fervor and the furor over laws being pumped out of the Arizona State Legislature such as SB 1070, she and her colleagues stay busy. "SB 1070 was sold to the public as a border enforcement measure, but it is more about interior enforcement,"

Soler says. "It's about people being stopped miles from the border and for unconstitutional reasons. SB 1070 was superficially reassuring the public, but it has nothing do with security along the border."

Although the law was upheld in part by the US Supreme Court and allows people to be stopped under a "reasonable suspicion" that they're in the United States illegally, Soler says the key unanswered question is "What is a reasonable suspicion?"

Because what may constitute reasonable suspicion was undefined, it is left up to individual law officers and their agencies. "What [police] rely on is the [suspect's] ability to speak English," Soler says. Even though people may be in the United States legally yet lack documents, "these people are at risk for being abused for a long period of time while the government figures it out."

Soler describes a case in which a young man was stopped and arrested for allegedly not having a driver's license. When the license was later produced, the officer called to apologize, telling the victim that "if he didn't make the arrest, he would lose his job. Not having a driver's license is one of the primary reasons for stopping [people] for 'reasonable suspicion.'"

In another case, a young boy was stopped while riding a bicycle and detained because he didn't have Arizona identification. The officer told the boy it was against the law not to have identification. "This is the life now for immigrants," Soler says. "If you are a person of color, you are going to be asked questions about your perceived immigration status." Because of SB 1070, police are now "mandated to do this. It goes against everything that this country is about."

Although SB 1070 is now in effect in Arizona, it runs counter to the Bill of Rights provisions that became part of the US Constitution, Soler says. "Citizens and noncitizens are entitled to be treated fairly under the law. When people are stopped for the color of their skin, it violates the equal treatment guarantee under the Fourteenth Amendment."

Soler says the ACLU and the Department of Justice have sued Sheriff Arpaio because of the way SB 1070 is being enforced. "There is no effort by the state to train officers not to engage in racial profiling," she notes, adding that ironically, "There is no way to enforce the law without racially profiling. This is what happens when you give police this kind of authority."

The ultimate result of the law, then, she says, is "to perpetuate a fear that the border is out of control," which is not the case. "Crime data and statistics don't support" the assertion that migrants have brought a crime wave. "Undocumented people don't commit crimes at a higher rate than other groups," she says.

Rather than being reviled, migrants should be recognized for the contributions they make to the state and national economy, Soler says. Arizona may have had as many as five hundred thousand undocumented workers, but that number is now probably about a hundred thousand, she says. "Most experts attribute the drop to the economy, not increased enforcement. It does cost money to educate immigrant children, but their contributions far outweigh the costs."

Migrants come across the border because they are given jobs, but then are singled out by law officers for maltreatment. "There are no lives for these people. There isn't a commonsense approach to helping twelve million people become legal. There is no process that helps them do that," she says. "There is no appetite for that." The challenge facing Congress is "to create an immigration process that helps people become citizens. The Supreme Court fell short. That is a problem."

★  ★  ★

In the eyes of people such as Spencer, Pearce, and Arpaio, border security has been a wholesale failure. I want to see for myself, so I go to the Border Patrol offices in Tucson, which has the highest concentration of border agents anywhere in the country. For several days I will get an inside look at border security, first at the Nogales port of entry then as part of a night patrol when Border Patrol agents arrest seventeen Mexicans who crossed into the United States just hours before.

# 10

# THE PORT AT NOGALES

᠅

**A** display case in the lobby of the US Border Patrol's Tucson Sector office contains an array of weapons and other items taken from apprehended migrants, such things as carefully made caps with a fake US Border Patrol logo and chunks of carpet with laces. Known as "carpet booties," they are tied to the bottom of boots and shoes by border crossers so as not to leave telltale footprints in the soft dirt and sand. The contents of the case illustrate some of the daily threats and problems faced by the several thousand agents who work the sprawling Tucson Sector—ground zero of the Border Patrol's battle against illegal immigration and drug smuggling.

The sense of a region under siege grows as I talk with Brent Cagen, a Border Patrol public affairs officer, while we roll south on Interstate 19 in a Border Patrol vehicle. "Down here you either love the Border Patrol or hate the Border Patrol," Cagen says. "There is no middle ground." Like others I've encountered in the agency, Cagen likes to talk about numbers: the sector covers 90,000 square miles and has 262 miles of border, most of which have some sort of fence. The areas that don't have fencing don't need it, he says, because they're mountaintops or other "environmental obstacles." While the sector agents found the remains of more than 175 dead in the desert during the previous year, they also saved some 550 migrants who were injured or near death from dehydration. About 112,000 migrants were caught in the sector during the period, about one-third of all immigrants detained along the Mexican border. For the same period, almost one million pounds of marijuana were confiscated.

About twenty miles north of the Mexico line, we wheel into the large Border Patrol checkpoint on the northbound lane of the interstate, one of eleven such "tactical" checkpoints scattered throughout the region. The checkpoints are a secondary screen of vehicles for drug and human smuggling, the first being at the port of entry, and make it difficult for collaborators who carry people and drugs across the border to be picked up at prearranged locations deeper in the United States. Although some rural checkpoints have only several agents, this one is housed under a large, arching fabric roof where cars and trucks are directed though orange cones past drug-sniffing dogs and questioning agents.

"They look for things that may be out of place, that don't fit the circumstances," Cagen says. "There have been incidents of individuals being aggressive. Anything can happen at any time." As we watch the traffic, a large, white panel truck pulls up beside us that contains an X-ray scanner that can detect organic material, such as marijuana, hidden inside vehicles. Cagen then points to the highway overpass nearby, where a tower supports a video and infrared camera that scans the surrounding terrain for migrants skirting the checkpoint by foot.

Back in our vehicle, I ask Cagen about a deportation policy that angers so many human rights activists and that sends people back across the border at locations far from where they were picked up. It's the Alien Transfer Exit Program, he says, and is not meant to break up families, as some have charged. The idea is "to take an individual out of the hands of the smuggling organizations and put them where they can get back to their homes safely," he says. The thinking behind the program is that when a migrant is apprehended and returned to the nearest port of entry, he or she goes back to the same people who tried to get them across initially. "We will never separate a family. We do everything we can to help families stay together. Parents and children will never be separated. That's not the business we're in."

Close to the border, we veer off the interstate and head to the Mariposa commercial port of entry and stop at the headquarters of the Nogales Station, home to some eight hundred agents, nearly a quarter of all the agents in the sector. This is where I had crossed the border months earlier with the human rights activists of No More Deaths to meet with recently deported migrants at the El Comedor dining hall. The Nogales Station is home to the agency's foot patrols, all-terrain-vehicle teams, and the traditional horse patrols. Cagen says that when the US Border Patrol began in 1924, agents needed to have a horse and a rifle to be hired. That's no longer the case, certainly.

We step into the "radio room," a darkened chamber where a half-dozen people sit at a long desk and monitor dozens of screens showing a myriad of camera angles at various locations along the border. These images are being broadcast by the many tower-mounted cameras that are part of the border surveillance system. From inside the room, the operators control the cameras much like a video game, swiveling around and zooming in and out. If someone spots suspicious activity, the radio room operators contact agents in the field about what they're seeing and where it is happening.

Downstairs we meander through what once was the Nogales Processing Center, an eerily empty, cavernous concrete room divided into cages and corridors made of floor-to-ceiling chain-link fencing. When illegal crossings peaked less than a decade ago, this is where hundreds of migrants were held each day before being deported or jailed. Because the volume of captured migrants has dropped so drastically in recent years, the processing center has been moved to Tucson. It is easy to imagine these now-empty cages packed with desperate, weary faces of people wondering what fate awaits them.

Outside in the harsh light of the Nogales morning, I am brought back to reality when I am handed a paintball gun by George Schmid, a Border Patrol captain. The gun looks like a toy, until Schmid explains that it is the patrol's weapon now being used "instead of going lethal" in response to the frequent attacks on border agents. There were 170 assaults on Border Patrol agents in the past year, he says, including the "rocking" incidents in which people on the Mexican side of the border heave rocks and chunks of concrete at agents. Such rocks smash through vehicle windshields, causing serious injuries, Cagen says. Earlier he had shown me how the agency was welding protective wire mesh over vehicle windshields and windows.

The plastic ball ammunition used by the Border Patrol is filled with pepper spray, an irritant meant to distract and deter "aggressively assaulting individuals," Schmid says. "The best place to hit somebody is the skin," since the balls sting but don't penetrate the skin. "I've been rocked," Schmid says darkly, "but people being apprehended are in danger [from flying rocks] as well. Our goal is not to kill anybody." Schmid hands me the gun then points to a metal cutout of a human figure. I aim and fire. A burst of powder pops on the dirt beyond the target. I shoot until I can hit the target consistently.

Nonlethal responses to rocking and other confrontations along the border have become an issue following shooting deaths of people on the Mexican side of the border by US agents. One was in Nogales just two months earlier. According to various news reports and details from the Nogales Police Department, city police and border agents responded to calls late on the night of October 10, 2012, that a couple of Mexican teenagers had tossed a bundle of marijuana over the border fence near downtown.

Nogales police arrived quickly and apparently were pursuing the suspects when Border Patrol agents arrived. People who had gathered on the Mexican side began throwing rocks. When they refused to stop, one agent apparently opened fire, killing a sixteen-year-old Nogales, Sonora, boy, Jose Antonio Elena Rodriguez. The shooting death set off a firestorm of complaints from local and national officials in Mexico after a Mexican medical examiner reported that the boy was shot multiple times in the back. It was not the first time such shootings had occurred. In 2010 a fifteen-year-old boy was killed by a border agent shooting across the border from El Paso into Juárez. In 2011 a border agent shot and killed a man as he climbed the border fence in south-eastern Arizona after the man had apparently been caught with about fifty pounds of marijuana. In all, twenty people have been killed by US agents along the border since early 2010, according to an October 2013 report by the *Republic* newspaper in Phoenix.

Back in our vehicle, Cagen negotiates the rugged gravel hills just west of downtown Nogales, not far from the spot of the Rodriguez shooting a couple of months earlier. As we enter a west Nogales neighborhood, Cagen points to a turquoise-painted house where agents recently found a tunnel that had been burrowed under the border fence and that originated in a building on the Mexican side. He motions to the doorway of a building where the tunnel was found. "The US will backfill the tunnel to the Mexican border," he says. "We won't go onto their side, but typically they [backfill] the same day we do it." Dozens of tunnels are found every year along the border, and are increasingly sophisticated with lighting and ventilation, many of them along the California-Mexico border.

## Port of Entry

Juan Osorio is a Mexican-born American who oversees one of the busiest ports of entry along the US-Mexico border. Osorio takes his job seriously, and since he grew up in here, treats the port like his hometown neighborhood. "When I was a kid, you didn't have this wait time," he says, as we watch a glut of cars and pickup trucks inch their way through the crowded inspection lanes. Although most cars are waved through after a cursory glance by agents, many are waved aside for inspection. The driver and passengers must go to a waiting room until the inspection is complete. Osorio and I watch a dozen blue-uniformed agents look under hoods, peer below dashboards, lift rear seats, and rummage through trunks.

The wait to cross the border can be long, Osorio says, because there are some fifteen thousand crossings here each day and the decades-old port was not built to accommodate this volume. Most people cross the border to shop, he says, since the American products are much cheaper in the United States, and Mexican-made goods that Americans want are much cheaper on the Mexican side. Some of those crossing are students, he says, who are American-born but whose families live in Nogales on the Mexican side of the border, where the cost of living is lower. "It's a community thing." Some Americans crossing the border live in the United States but work as managers in the maquiladoras, the factories on the Mexican side, he says.

"The ports are a gateway to the economies of both countries," Osorio says, and in the midst of all this activity, "we have people trying to bring in narcotics and illegal immigrants." After the terrorist attacks of 9/11 and the dramatic rise in drug cartel crimes along the border, the mood at the ports of entry is vastly different from past years, Osorio says. "It's not the same feeling we used to have," he says, when people knew one another and they moved across the border easily. "People say, 'Why [are you checking me]? You know me,'" Osorio says. "We have to make sure nothing critical gets by us. That is what people have a hard time understanding. We're much more vigilant." Inspectors routinely ask several questions, he says, and conduct "more of an interview, because you never know." The level of smuggling requires tougher methods, he says. "[If] you elevate the crime, you [must] increase enforcement."

Osorio says technology is good but can't replace an experienced officer. "Our best tool is an officer's experience and intuition. You can have all of the technology and it doesn't do [the job] as well." Agents pick up on little clues, he says. "When you have an officer ask some questions, he wants to see how truthful you're being."

For example, if a person is returning to Mexico from the United States, he will be asked where he went shopping. If the reply is to the Walmart in Tucson, the person may be asked why he didn't just go to the Walmart in Nogales, Arizona. If the person stumbles for an answer, that triggers suspicion. Sometimes child seats are put in cars to make the drivers look like they have family. This might prompt an officer to ask, "How many children do you have?" If the person hesitates to answer, it is suspicious. "That's how we catch people in lies," Osorio says.

Osorio takes me to the pedestrian entry where people must pass through a turnstile of steel bars to an open space where agents check documents. With thousands of people crossing back and forth each day, most of the work is routine, he says. But then something catches his eye. Several men, whom Osorio notices are not Mexican, are stopped by an agent. The men claim to be from India and are asking for political asylum, he says.

Moments later we climb a maze of steps to the port of entry offices and yet another room filled with video screens showing the views from various vantage points being monitored by officers. On one of the empty screens in the room, Osorio cues up a video of a rock-throwing incident, saying that he wants me to see how dangerous they are.

In it, a handful of people charge the port at the same spot where he and I were standing moments earlier and hurl rocks. A rock the size of a brick hits an unsuspecting officer, glancing off his head and knocking him to the pavement. Osorio says the rock throwers were not attacking the officers but a car that had been involved in a hit-and-run incident earlier that evening. The driver was fleeing an angry Mexican crowd.

Osorio shows me another video, this of a human-smuggling incident at the pedestrian entry turnstile. In the middle of the night, a couple pushes a small child through the bars, then leaves the child to sit alone on the pavement. Moments later, a young man appears and takes the child by the hand. Just as he turns to leave, US border officers grab the man and child.

Down another corridor and through a security door, we enter the central processing unit of the port, where people apprehended at the port are kept for questioning and held for detention or deportation. Two dozen people are waiting in a large, wire mesh cage, including a handful of undocumented Mexicans who were stopped as they tried to slip back into Mexico from the United States. When I ask Osorio why he bothers with such people since they are leaving the country, he says that some may be criminals trying to escape capture and punishment. Undocumented migrants are checked against crime data banks for arrest warrants anywhere in the United States. If the port were to let a criminal felon escape, they would be challenged and asked, "Why didn't you stop him?"

Among those being questioned by the immigration officers are the Indian men seeking asylum that we saw some minutes earlier. They are on a three-way, online conversation with a federal translator who speaks Hindu. The officer is trying to ascertain the identity and details of the men's history to determine what can and should be done with them. Such encounters are not unusual, Osorio says, noting that Mexicans are not the only people trafficked into the United States through the Mexican border. "They're coached as to what to say," he says, indicating that such trafficking of foreigners is a sophisticated and widespread operation.

## Ambos Nogales

Arturo Garino, the mayor of Nogales, Arizona, remembers picking vegetables in the fields south of Tucson with his parents. "As a child, I traveled with buses that would pick up workers from Mexico and take them to Green Valley," a community about thirty miles to the north. It was part of the now-defunct Bracero Program, Garino says. "It was a very successful program," because it helped people on both sides of the border. Mexicans earned money and Arizona farmers had their crops harvested. "Nobody left the bus," he says of the pickers. "They all came back." There was little or no illegal immigration then, Garino notes, and the fence along the border was just five strands of barbed wire. "That was it. It was basically nothing."

Life along the border changed in the late 1960s and early 1970s. "That's when the drugs picked up," Garino says, but even then, "Nobody paid much attention. Downtown Nogales was booming. It was a lot of fun. You couldn't find a parking space. Then 9/11 came along. Now, if one person is shot, you learn about it on Fox and CNN."

Garino blames the buildup of security along the border on the climate of fear created by Arizona politicians, not a growing crime rate. "Six or seven years ago, they started using the border for political gains. That really gave us a problem." Their campaign messages were simple: "Elect me, and I'll stop what is going on at the border," Garino says. "But [crime] was worse in the 1980s," Garino says. He blames US senator John McCain and Arizona governor Jan Brewer, among others. "Brewer and some of the senators started this. But there is nothing to control." Garino's message to the Phoenix politicos: "Do your job over there and let us take care of our issues here."

The problems faced by Nogales, Arizona, and the surrounding Santa Cruz County are not of the city and county residents' making, Garino says. "We have a lot of tunnels in Santa Cruz County, but we find them. Why? We have a demand for the drugs and illegal aliens," a demand that comes from Phoenix and the rest of the United States. "You want to have soldiers?" he asks. "Then put them in your city. You've already created a culture of fear so people don't want to come here."

Fear keeps people from Nogales, and the town is suffering badly, just like the Mexican town Nogales directly across the border, Garino says. All border communities are battling an image problem, he says. "We all fight the same perception." Ironically, the massive presence of border enforcement now in the town "makes us a very safe community" despite people's fears. The only Americans who cross the border do so mostly for the inexpensive dental care. "There is no more fun and play."

"If we had a better government at the state level," Garino believes, there would be twice as much economic activity in the region than there is now. Nogales is a gateway for the region and "part of the global economy." Mexican agricultural products found in grocery stores throughout the United States come through Nogales. "Once you get people thinking about trade, we will eliminate those politicians who started the culture of fear. Nine-eleven didn't start [the fear]. There were other forces at play that caused it."

Immigration reform can help by increasing the number of guest worker and student visas, Garino says. It will help the United States by attracting the best and the brightest to the country. Let students "get a degree from the University of Arizona, then send them back to Mexico?" he asks. "Come on. They should stay here." Reforming the current visa situation will take some work, he says, because "they're going to have to remove the political hacks" who have created the anti-immigrant fear. "We should open up [immigration] a little more, but it's not happening in Washington. I hope it gets done. I hope we do something."

Garino opposes amnesty, saying it encourages illegal immigration, but supports a pathway to US citizenship for undocumented migrants already in the country via military service and other methods. "It's time for [Congress] to sit down and do this," because most of the migrants who would be affected "have jobs to go to already."

The mood of the country has shifted on immigration, and Garino predicts that the critical role of the Hispanic vote in the 2012 election will spur politicians into action. Those opposing immigration reform will be punished politically, he says. "Politicians tap into something they hope will take them somewhere. If it's good, they run with it. But once it fails, they don't want to have anything to do with it. That's why immigration [reform] will be an issue."

I point out that many undocumented migrants are self-deporting, which supports the argument that some make against immigration reform.

"A lot of people are going back because they feel they're not wanted, that they can get stopped anytime," Garino replies. Instead of subjecting so many people to arrest, a temporary worker visa program needs to be reinstituted. "I worked in the fields because I needed to," he says. He earned money for school, books, and clothes, and now is the mayor of a border town. "I hope people understand how important Mexico is to the economic health of the nation."

## Sheriff Estrada

"It's sad because I can't go home," says Tony Estrada, the sheriff of Santa Cruz County. Although Estrada was born in Mexico, he can't return because of his position as commander of a force of deputies that patrol this rural county, a major route for drugs and migrants. From his newly built offices on a hill overlooking the town of Nogales, Estrada is nostalgic about how life here once was. "It's changed. We're a major corridor," he says "It's a dangerous atmosphere." Drug smuggling is the biggest threat, Estrada says, and "all communities have a different threat level." One such community is Rio Rico, where Border Patrol agent Brian Terry was killed just a couple of years earlier, and another is Arivaca, where young Brisenia Flores and her father, Raul, were shot and killed by border vigilantes.

Estrada is a lifelong law officer, having worked twenty years with the Nogales Police Department before running for sheriff, a position he's held since 1992. He was reelected in November 2012 to a sixth four-year term and oversees a country with a population of about forty-seven thousand. About a thousand Border Patrol agents are in the county, he says. Across the border is Nogales, Sonora, with more than three hundred thousand people. "In your backyard you have a Third World country," so it's expected that people and drugs will come across.

"There's always been drugs and illegals crossing the border," he says, but the mid-1990s was a turning point. "In 1995 we started to see people rush the ports," meaning that they would force their way across by foot or in vehicles. That same year the first underground tunnel for drug smuggling was found. "It was discovered in a church. Since then, seventy or eighty tunnels have been discovered," he says. Drugs and people are smuggled in Nogales because only a fence separates the two towns, allowing people to simply climb the fence and drop down the other side and be on their way. "There is no buffer zone here."

Once cross-border crime rose, Nogales installed better lighting, which helped thwart some of the crime. But then "we started finding dead bodies in the desert," most of whom had been shot during what he called "drug rip-offs." Checkpoints on the major roads "pushed people further out into the remote canyons," making rural areas more dangerous. Most encounters with smugglers are incidental, he admits. "The cartel wants to get their product to Phoenix. They want as little contact with law enforcement as possible. It's bad for business."

Terry's death was the result of one such drug rip-off, he says, which explains why the suspected killers were armed. But such rip-offs also affect many Mexican migrants coming across the desert. "They're lied to about the danger they're in," he says. The coyotes who lead the migrant groups "are human predators. They mislead these people to make money. The women are raped. There's a lot of activity in the remote areas. They are victimized so much, but this is their only hope, so they take the risk. I'm saddened that these people can be so cruel. We're seeing a new breed of cruel, insensitive people. It's turned ugly. There is no value to human life."

Estrada dislikes the towering, rusted steel fence that divides the Mexican and the American Nogales, referred to as Ambos (both) Nogales. It's a constant reminder of how much times have changed. "I see it as an affront between two friendly neighbors. The US took its eye off of Mexico for too long. They didn't work with Mexico on some issues that they share as neighbors. They're having to make up for lost time and missed opportunities."

The massive presence of border security personnel has more than addressed the concerns raised by Arizona's SB 1070, he says. "The border here is safe and secure, but it is not sealed," he says, because the economies of both countries depend on trade with each other. But, he concedes, that will never satisfy everyone. "All that's going to make some people happy is when nothing passes. But if you seal off the border, then you choke the economy."

The border will never be sealed as long as the demand for drugs exists, Estrada says. "There is a strong demand. We've got a serious issue with drugs [in America]. It's a fluid, dynamic border, and you have a large pool of people who are willing to carry it across." Many young Mexicans came north to the border when US companies opened factories in Mexico after NAFTA was approved. "People came here to find jobs. Now, a lot of young people are involved in the drug trade.

It's an enticement based on need. That is a challenge we will continue to have."

Who is to blame for the massive drug trade? I ask. "We can point a finger both ways, to the consumer and the provider," Estrada says.

Estrada is no fan of SB 1070 and says it has the potential to cause a lot of problems in Santa Cruz County. "I opposed 1070 and I was vocal about it. When 1070 raised its ugly head, I feared they would want us to enforce [stricter] immigration [laws]. We can't afford to do that," he says, because of the high number of migrants who are captured in his county. "We got blindsided by the feds," who told the county to jail the immigrant detainees, Estrada says.

But the Santa Cruz County facilities are far too small. "We can't afford to do immigration enforcement. They thought only about one group, the Mexicans," he says of the drafters of SB 1070. "It's racial profiling. It was inevitable. It's already being done in Maricopa County. It is terrible. Hopefully all of that will go away. It is not the appropriate approach to the problem. There have to be ways to go about it that are fair."

With a sense of resignation and sadness, Estrada says, "things are never going to be the same again. It used to be the tourists would come over [to Nogales] to eat. You could buy a gallon of liquor" and take it back to the United States duty-free. "The draw now is dentistry and medicine." The changes have also altered the ethnic makeup of the town, he says. Korean merchants have recently opened up stores in Nogales, selling inexpensive clothes and other goods. "Who would have thought you'd see Koreans? They are providing a service," he concedes. "We're moving into the next chapter, and I don't know what that is."

## Lunch in Nogales

Not far from Estrada's office is a Nogales landmark restaurant, Zulas, which serves a mix of American and Mexican food, and world-class homemade apple pie à la mode. There I meet with lifelong resident

Melina Papachoris, forty-three, the daughter of the restaurant's owners, George and Tita Papachoris. Melina is acutely aware of the climate of fear in the region, which exists for good reason. "I haven't crossed the borderline for three years," Papachoris says, even though she has friends and relatives on the Mexican side. "I am afraid of going across the line. I have no reason [to go]. It is a different world. If something happens, then what?"

Improved security in Nogales has helped, but not enough to convince her to once again visit the Mexican Nogales. "My grandparents lived across the line. Eventually, we brought them over here. A lot of the elementary students don't come across anymore," Papachoris says, explaining that she was an elementary school teacher for many years before leaving to help run the restaurant.

The tall fence that now divides the town has become a monument to fear and division, she says. "It contributes a lot to the fear that people have. My father used to have a Christmas party for the orphanage across the border. A few years back, that stopped. They wouldn't give us permission to bring the kids across." The climate of fear has also affected the restaurant. "We used to see a lot of tourists. They would take a pie back home. They've stopped coming. A lot of it has to do with the drug wars."

An incident that shook Papachoris occurred as she and her husband were in a car stopped at the port of entry waiting to drive into Mexico. Shooting erupted, directed at the car immediately in front of them. Officials on the Mexican side also started shooting. She later learned that the car in front of them was carrying cash into Mexico, presumably drug money. Then, the father of the restaurant's cashier was shot and nearly killed in a drive-by shooting.

The situation seems to be improving, she says. "You hear [of violence] less and less now, which is good." Better security "makes people safer, but things can happen. There has been a gradual decline [in violence]. For us it's not so bad. I think things are relaxing more. There was a lot more violence before. There's not so much now." After a pause, she adds, "Or people are getting used to it."

Unlike others who see the expanded Border Patrol as a burden, Papachoris says, "I'm fine with them. People get upset, but they would be more upset if harm came to them. I'd like to see more [agents]. They're here to protect us."

Papachoris takes a conservative approach to the immigration problem. As a teacher for fifteen years, she witnessed Mexican parents who come across the border to take advantage of US government services such as free education and food stamps. "There were many illegals who got benefits that I'm not receiving. They're here for a better life, but also so they don't have to work," she says. "There are hardworking people, but I saw it all the time. That's what they were coming for, not to work." Papachoris excuses herself, saying she has to get back to work.

After a helping of the restaurant's apple pie and vanilla ice cream, I head back to Tucson to join the Border Patrol agents on a night patrol for illegal migrants.

# II

# AND WE'RE THE BAD GUYS?

⚜

**It is mid-afternoon a couple of days later,** and again I roll south out of Tucson on Interstate 19 in a Border Patrol vehicle. I'm with Border Patrol agents Jeremy Copeland and Ricardo "Rico" Novoa at the beginning of a nighttime border patrol. We turn off the interstate and take a winding two-lane highway through the town of Arivaca and continue south toward the border, turning onto dirt roads and leaving civilization behind as we enter the Forest Service's Pajarita Wilderness Area.

The talk is of tracking migrants in these remote and rugged hills, valleys, and sandy washes. Some encounters are accidental, Copeland says, such as the time three men, each carrying fifty-pound bundles of marijuana, crossed the road in front of him. Another time, agents came across marks in the road made by a grass rake that a smuggler had used to cover the tracks of his group. Agents tracked the rake marks and made their arrests. More common because it is not so obvious is a "brush out," Copeland says, in which the last person in the group uses a leafy branch to sweep out the tracks. There are other tricks such as using fake cow hoofprints or horseshoe marks to cover the tracks, he says. Some have rolled tires across the dirt "to make it seem like the Border Patrol has been there already with a vehicle," he says.

Much of this is done by drug traffickers, Novoa says, who have been known to launch brick-sized bundles of drugs over border fences with large slingshots. Near the southeastern Arizona border town of Naco, agents discovered a catapult that heaved marijuana bales over the fence. "We don't see a ton of cocaine," Copeland adds. "We see mostly big bundles of marijuana."

We drive for an hour on dirt roads that wind over and around the hills, eventually coming to one of the Border Patrol's communication and video towers atop a high knoll that offers an unobstructed view toward the border, just a mile or so away, and to valleys west and south. The terrain is no friend to the Border Patrol. Though the mountains are not high, they're rugged, restricting the line of sight, and covered with brush. The valleys and washes are shallow but deep enough to provide hiding spots.

As we wind our way down a steep road, we encounter another agent in a white and green truck who has just climbed a nearby mound and identified a couple of spotters—men who work for the coyotes bringing people across—on an adjacent peak. The spotter's job is to track the movements of the Border Patrol and report when the area is clear to bring a group across. It is unsettling to know that we are being watched.

The sun sinks low as we continue along the winding dirt roads, dropping into gullies and around the tree- and brush-covered hills, until we eventually drive into the tiny border town of Sasabe. As we take a quick break at this border crossing in one of the loneliest sections of the Sonoran Desert, the red sun drops below the horizon. Sasabe is all but closed for the night, but things are about to get busy for us.

Copeland and Novoa receive a report of a large group of migrants moving northward just east of Sasabe, having just crossed the same road on which we were driving. Both agents have small radio receivers with earphones and are in constant contact with other agents in the area and operation supervisors.

We meet with another agent and drive north on State Road 286, the paved highway out of Sasabe, turning onto a dirt road that takes us deep into the remote Buenos Aires National Wildlife Refuge. Daylight fades as we bump along rugged roads that become little more than dirt tracks, our SUV hurtling headfirst into the darkness as we eat the roiling dust of the lead truck. Copeland monitors his GPS device while we struggle to match the map to the terrain we can barely see out the window, an impossible task in the dust and dark.

We are to rendezvous with a handful of other Border Patrol agents barreling to the same coordinates but from the opposite direction. The migrant group is being tracked by a truck somewhere out there with a telescoping mast mounted with an infrared camera and laser beam capabilities, Copeland says. It is similar to the vehicle and devices I saw a couple of months ago at the border security expo in El Paso. The mobile tower operator shoots a laser beam to the group and then calls out the group's precise coordinates.

As we clunk down washed-out roads and bounce up the side of gullies, the agents discuss whether we should douse our lights so as not to alert the migrants of our approach. Luckily, we keep the lights on. Copeland says we are only a couple of miles from the group now and closing in. A helicopter has been dispatched from Tucson and is hovering behind the hills of the nearby Las Guijas Mountains, waiting until the agents on the ground, including us, can get closer. A fixed-wing aircraft is also circling and monitoring the migrants' progress.

After making a number of mistaken turns, we eventually encounter several other Border Patrol vehicles. We're less than a mile from the migrants now, who are moving north of us, Copeland says. The helicopter has moved in and is circling the group, hoping it will stop moving. Each of the agents is armed with a handgun and handcuffs, and at least one carries an assault rifle. With small flashlights in hand, we hustle over the rugged terrain toward the helicopter, which is now circling the migrants, who have hunkered down in a hillside ravine. The thud-thud of the chopper blades fills the night air.

Cactus thorns pierce pant legs and prick the skin as we scramble over and around the hills, slip down sandy washes, and clamber up the other side. Copeland calls out that we have less than a half-mile to go, but it seems to take forever as we hustle across the darkened terrain. I am not the only one puffing for breath.

Finally we crest a hill where the helicopter hovers, the migrants caught in its powerful floodlight. The agents split into two groups, one circling to the left and below the group, and the other to the right and above it. Copeland and I wait and watch from a distance, because of the potential for violence. The helicopter crew initially counted nineteen in the group, but when the agents close in, there are only seventeen. The missing two are the coyotes, Copeland says. Since we're still close to the border, they're making a run for it.

Since no one tries to flee as the agents secure the group, the helicopter rises and circles over Copeland and me toward the high foothills to chase the two coyotes. In moments the two men are spotted and lighted. But the chopper lifts and circles back.

"Aren't you going after the two escapees?" I ask.

Copeland shrugs in frustration. There aren't enough agents on hand to give chase.

Minutes later the migrants file down the slope, many handcuffed one to another, their shadowy silhouettes barely visible. Copeland and I fall in behind after they pass. Most are in their twenties and early thirties, and two are women. They're all identically dressed in camouflaged, military-style cargo pants and camouflaged hooded sweatshirts, and they carry camouflaged backpacks loaded with food, drinks, and extra clothes. Each also wears well-constructed "carpet booties" that are much more sophisticated than what I saw earlier in the display case. The trip back to the trucks is much easier, since we walk along the well-worn trail that the migrants had walked less than an hour earlier, which we did not use as we chased them.

After thirty minutes, we're back at the vehicles where the agents have the migrants sit down so they can be assessed. Novoa and I talk with some of the group about their journey. Most are from Mexico

City and six are related. Four have been living in Queens, New York, for the past few years, working in restaurants and elsewhere. They are on their way back to New York after having returned to Mexico City to take care of family business. They have jobs waiting for them in New York, they say, and will probably try to cross again, since they only pay their coyote guides once they reach their destinations.

As the group sits on the ground, quietly talking, I ask about the carpet booties. These are hand-sewn cloth boots with carpeted bottoms and sturdy uppers with laces, clearly crafted for a trek. They explain that the booties and the other supplies were purchased from migrant outfitters in Altar, Sonora, a town about thirty miles due south of where we are now. The booties cost ninety Mexican pesos, or about seven dollars a pair. Moving people across the border into the United States is a thriving business in Mexico.

The group is loaded into the cramped compartments fitted onto the beds of the Border Patrol pickup trucks and are driven into the night. Copeland, Novoa, and I climb into our vehicle and head back to Tucson Sector headquarters, where the migrants will be taken as well. Those who have been captured for the first time will most likely be processed and deported after a few days. Those for whom this is their second or third immigration violation will be placed in what is known as Operation Streamline, the special federal program that puts these offenders in prison from one or two months to a year.

## Not Like Selling Groceries

A couple of days before my night patrol, I talk with Andy Adame, a veteran Border Patrol special operations supervisor at the Tucson Sector. As opportunities for jobs in the United States grew, and as increasing numbers of Mexicans decided to cross the border illegally, the drug cartels killed or pushed out the groups that once controlled the border crossing business. Things got violent. "We started seeing rapes, beatings, and robberies," Adame says. "Last year we found a guy tied to a tree. It was a miracle that a helicopter spotted him." The flood of illegal border crossings also gave rise to the *bajadores*, the gangs that attack migrants, the so-called rip crews. "They're animals of opportunity," Adame says. "They rob people and rape the women. That's what they do."

Research reveals that about half of the migrants crossing into the United States come from Mexico City and the Mexican states of Oaxaca, Puebla, Sonora, and Guerrero, Adame says. Another 20 percent come from Central American countries, primarily Guatemala. "A lot of them have never heard of the dangers" of crossing the border. "Their perception is that there is plenty of water in the desert," based on the claims by the coyotes that the humanitarian groups place water drops everywhere. "It may help save some lives," Adame says of the water drops, "but it also creates a false impression." The water drops are not always helpful, according to some migrants, Adame says. The migrants who come across the water drops are usually lost, having been separated from their groups. "They say they tried to drink the water, but it was too hot. And even if they drink the water, they're still lost."

While the migrants always carry food and water, they should also carry cell phones and hand-held mirrors in case they become lost, Adame says, but few do. "Every agent has seen the pain and suffering that goes with illegal immigration. Coyotes can drop people off anywhere they like," in the remote regions along the border. "They don't see a life there. They see a commodity. When [agents] show up, those who are lost want to hug us . . . and we're the bad guys."

Arizona has become the major corridor for illegal immigration because almost 75 percent of the Arizona border, as well as most of Arizona itself, is either public land or is on the land of the Tohono O'odham reservation. The reservation is a "weak point" for enforcement and therefore a concentrated conduit for illegal immigration.

Today's border enforcement is vastly improved over what Adame experienced in San Diego in the 1980s as a young recruit with the Border Patrol. There he regularly saw thousands of people cross an unsecured border. "You'd see large masses of people coming across all night long, 365 days a year. I was twenty-two, and nobody cared about the Border Patrol back then. We'd catch a hundred people per night. Back then, with only a chain link fence, it took eight seconds to cross the border. When we came up with something new, they'd come up with something. With a new fence, it now takes about a minute [to climb over]. The border is as secure as it has ever been. Is there more to do? Absolutely."

The job of an agent continues to be dangerous, Adame says. "People used to sit on top [of the fence] and they'd rock you. Now we have pepper balls. It stops the rock throwers and we can de-escalate the situation. It beats getting shot." He pauses for a moment, then says, "Patrolling the border is not like selling groceries."

## Cases of Corruption

As Adame suggests, Border Patrol agents are on the front lines of what can be a dangerous and deadly war that battles the illegal importation of people and drugs. The job demands commitment and resilience, qualities that not all agents have. As such, the Border Patrol has been hit with its own crime problem, in part because the patrol has been effective at intercepting drugs crossing the border. Cartels are being hit and have responded by enticing a few agents into helping them.

In December 2005 an agent was caught on camera taking a bundle of marijuana from the back of a smuggler's pickup truck. The incident was captured on film by the Arizona Highway Patrol officers who had stopped the pickup on a road south of Tucson. A patrol officer let his vehicle's video camera roll while he and another officer chased the driver and a passenger into the brush. A Border Patrol agent had been called in to secure drugs, and thinking he was alone, helped himself to a bundle worth about $20,000, calmly waiting for the officers to return.

In the spring of 2011 another Border Patrol agent was caught with more than seven hundred pounds of marijuana in his truck with an estimated street value of nearly $400,000. The thirty-four-year-old agent was arrested while on duty in a remote stretch of the border near San Luis, a town south of Yuma, Arizona. Federal prosecutors said the agent set off sensors along the border, and when other Border Patrol agents arrived, they found the agent's truck backed up against the fence, where marijuana was being handed over by Mexican smugglers.

In early December 2012 a Border Patrol agent was stopped in the same region and also caught loading marijuana into his truck. According to reports, a remote camera caught the agent as he pulled up to the border fence, where three men on the Mexican side handed duffel bags to the agent, who loaded them into his truck and drove away. The agent was arrested and charged with drug trafficking. In the affidavit, the agent reportedly quipped, "I'm fucked. You guys got me on video."

Admittedly, the number of corruption cases pursued by the agency is very small compared to the overall size of the Customs and Border Protection agency, with nearly sixty thousand employees, of which the Border Patrol is part. Though 130 agents have been arrested and charged with crimes over the past eight years, the CBP agency had more than 600 "active" cases under investigation as of June 2011, according to the *Arizona Daily Star*.

Some involve human rights abuses. In 2008 two agents were accused of stopping four Mexican men on the Tohono O'odham Indian reservation and making them eat some of the marijuana they were carrying. The Mexican detainees were apparently forced to strip down to their underwear despite nighttime temperatures dropping to forty degrees. The agents reportedly set fire to the Mexicans' belongings and told them to run into the desert. The agents will later be convicted of violating the detainees' human rights.

Agency corruption could be much worse, some say, given its rapid expansion, since hiring managers may not have conducted adequate background checks. Others argue that the Mexican drug cartels are conducting an all-out campaign to bribe and entice agents into facilitating the shipment of drugs and people across the border. Despite that, and given the size and scope of the Border Patrol, the incidents of corruption remain low.

## Revolving Door

Apprehending people and drugs coming across the border may be the most notorious role of the Border Patrol, but it is only the opening act to a detainee drama that ends with jail or deportation. Next door to the Tucson Sector headquarters is the Border Patrol's processing center, where apprehended migrants like the ones I encountered on the night patrol are taken to be fingerprinted, interviewed, and categorized for either deportation or to face federal charges and a trial.

Danielle Suarez, a Border Patrol supervisory agent, accompanies me through the center, where we watch some two hundred migrants being processed. When migrants are brought here, their backpacks are tagged and placed on a wall of metal shelving.

The center is a large, heavily fortified circular facility divided into two semicircles. Migrants wait in an outer ring of rooms to be called for their screening interview. Many are wrapped in tin-foil-like blankets they're given to fend off the cold, and are called individually to be interviewed by agents at an inner ring of desks. Behind the agents is a supervisor who oversees the operation and signs off on each migrant's assessment. I am prohibited from taking pictures, Suarez explains, to protect the agents from being identified and possibly becoming victims of retaliation or intimidation.

Each migrant's information is run through federal crime databases, Suarez explains. Those lacking prior offenses are charged with a misdemeanor. The agency has its own immigration court where the migrants are adjudicated, then deported. "We hold court here," Suarez says, "so we don't have to transfer custody" to another federal agency. The migrants are then put on a bus and taken to ports of entry far from Tucson "so they can't just immediately hook up with their smuggler and cross again."

Those caught carrying drugs or who have been caught crossing before are funneled into Operation Streamline. Previously, the agency simply deported people, Suarez says. "It was a quick way to process people, but it was not very effective [in stopping illegal immigration].

There were no consequences [to illegal entry]. It was not having an effect. We found [Operation Streamline] was most effective for second- and third-time offenders."

## Operation Streamline

The DeConcini Federal Courthouse is an imposing structure in downtown Tucson. Every weekday, year in and year out, hundreds of undocumented migrants are brought before the courts here in brisk, brief trials, with many sentenced to a year or more in federal prison after pleading guilty or being found so. The trials are open, so on a day in late October 2012 I enter a federal courtroom packed with appre- hended migrants wearing orange jumpsuits and gray shoes, their hands bound by chains that connect the cuffs on their hands and feet. Although I arrive fifteen minutes early, I am prevented from enter- ing the courtroom because these minutes before court sessions are reserved for the handful of local defense attorneys to meet with their clients, the charged migrants. It is the only time most migrants have to meet and consult with their defenders.

Once the courtroom doors open, the gears of justice begin to grind. The judge gavels the court into session and names are called, each migrant responding with a "*presente.*" As the judge conducts the session in English, his words are translated simultaneously for the migrants, who use the court's earphones. The first five migrants stand before the judge's bench and nod when asked if they understand that they have the right to remain silent and to request a full trial. The migrants routinely plead guilty to the misdemeanor charge of illegal entry into the United States, however, in exchange for the federal gov- ernment dropping the felony charge. Most of the cases I witness result in sentences of 150 to 180 days in jail. The illegal entry charge carries a sentence of up to 180 days in jail and a fine of $5,000. The entire pro- cess takes about five minutes.

The second group brought before the bench consists of seven men. The judge asks the defendants if they are pleading guilty of their own free will or if they have been coerced. They all say they're pleading guilty freely. The judge then sentences each to specific periods in jail, and in the case of one, allows the man to serve his jail time in Chicago so he can be visited by his family there, illustrating the widespread nature of the immigration problem.

A third group stands before the judge, and one is charged with a slightly different crime: aiding and abetting illegal entry. The man apparently was part of a network of human smugglers and worked on the Arizona side of the border, having been caught driving a pickup truck with four undocumented migrants. The judge sentences the man to forty-five days in jail, over the objections of the man's attorney, who complains that his client has a medical problem that has not been addressed by the private company that operates the jail. The judge replies that the medical issue is not life-threatening and sends the man off to serve his time.

Another two defendants, a man and a woman, face up to a year in prison and a $100,000 fine for being caught carrying marijuana into the country. The woman had a fake Arizona birth certificate and the man was caught a week earlier with about twenty kilograms, or forty-four pounds, of marijuana, wandering in the desert with two others who were also carrying bundles of marijuana. The defendant tells the judge, "We were forced. They threatened me with a pistol," and says he was watched from the distant hills to ensure that he carried the drugs.

The judge asks why the defendant didn't drop the bundle when he was out of sight of the cartel minders. The defendant says nothing and sits down. The judge then sentences the woman to ninety-five days in jail and attends to the cases of two others before returning to the marijuana-carrying migrant. The defendant suddenly changes his story and says, "I was carrying the marijuana voluntarily. I wanted to come here to work." The judge presses the man for an explanation. The defendant says that by agreeing to carry the drugs, he would not have to pay the $2,000 or more that he would have been charged to be smuggled across the border. "I was looking for a reduction in the smuggling fee," the man says. The judge indicates that he appreciates the man's honesty, then sentences him to 180 days in jail.

There are other courtrooms and additional sessions that I observe, and many of the cases are much more complicated. One man is sent to be tried in federal court in Minnesota after having been deported in California and caught after he reentered. Another was caught at a port of entry with fake identification. Another was caught carrying methamphetamine. Six others are charged with two counts of illegal entry, and the judge advises them to plead guilty to the lesser crime in order to receive a shorter sentence. A group of four caught with bundles of marijuana are charged with the crime of intent to distribute a controlled substance, and the judge suggests that they plead guilty to the lesser charge of simple marijuana possession. Most do.

## A Waste of Money

Across the courtyard behind the federal courthouse are the offices of Heather Williams, a top federal public defender for Operation Streamline. An eighteen-year veteran of the defender's office, Williams is a vocal critic of the federal prosecuting program, calling it "an obscene waste of taxpayers' money."

The United States is one of the few countries that make illegal entry a criminal rather than a civil violation, Williams says, and these laws have been on the books since the 1930s. Most countries punish illegal immigration with administrative penalties, Williams explains, where offenders also can be jailed for up to eighteen months or two years before being deported. But the result is not a criminal conviction. When three Americans hikers were arrested inside Iran near the Iraq border in July 2009, they were charged as spies, not for entering the country illegally, Williams notes. Some European countries, however, such as Spain and Italy, have recently enacted criminal in addition to administrative penalties for illegal immigration.

Williams has visited the Border Patrol's processing center in Tucson, which is the source of the migrants she and her colleagues are asked to defend with little or no time to prepare. "The smell," she says of the center, which is like a stuffy gymnasium, is something she can't forget. "The people there have been walking the desert for days and have not had a chance to clean up. It's humiliating. When you appear before the judge, you want to present yourself well," she says, but under the current arrangements, that's impossible. "We have to figure out a way to minimize the damage. There clearly is a need for immigration reform."

Williams acknowledges that reform will be difficult, because the current system has been tweaked so many times over the past decades. "It's incredibly complex," she says, "but it need not be so reactionary. We need to get serious about keeping families together, even in the cases of criminal context," noting that children of migrants born in the United States are essentially orphaned when their parents are deported. Immigration reform must address the realities in the United States, she says. "We depend on migrant labor, so why not make it easier?"

Williams is critical of Operation Streamline, because it does not solve the immigration problem. "The economy has had a far greater impact [on slowing illegal immigration] than Streamline ever will. People's motivation [to cross the border illegally] is out of desperation" for jobs and education, she says. "That kind of desperation is not accommodated in immigration law. Can you imagine the desperation?"

Current government border and immigration policy has the opposite effect of what is intended, Williams says. "Our immigration policy and the militarization of the border has kept a lot of people here. They're afraid to go back [to Mexico] because they can't get back in. So they end up staying here."

The post-9/11 era has generated undue fear of foreigners, she says. "Over time, the people south of the border have become the enemy. We needed an enemy, and the immigrant became it."

★ ★ ★

The polarization in Arizona and elsewhere in the United States over immigration and the border has created an ideological divide.

Solutions seem unreachable and compromise is a foreign concept. But a glimmer of hope appears when I learn about a small group at work in Douglas, Arizona, that has been building strong and beneficial ties for people on both sides of the border for a decade. The group's work is a modest yet inspiring example of what can be done. That is where I go.

# V

★ ★ ★

# BREWING A SOLUTION

12

# TO LEAVE OUR LAND IS TO SUFFER

⚜

**Café Justo (Just Coffee)** is a coffee-growing cooperative based in the town of Salvador Urbina in the southern Mexican state of Chiapas. The community sits on the lush rain-forest slopes of a towering volcano on the Guatemalan border, and as in Guatemala, the coffee produced here is renowned for its smooth taste and low acid content. The co-op celebrated ten years of existence in 2012 and has offices and a coffee-roasting and packing operation in Agua Prieta, Sonora, across the border from Douglas, Arizona.

When I learn that Tommy Bassett, director of the co-op's Just Trade Development Center, will lead a small group to Salvador Urbina for the co-op's anniversary celebration, I jump at the chance to go. The concept behind the co-op is simple: provide the coffee growers in this impoverished community with a better price for their annual harvest of high-quality coffee beans than they would otherwise get from the region's commercial coffee buyers, who offer take-it-or-leave-it prices. By selling their coffee to the co-op at substantially higher prices, the growers and their families earn more and are less likely to travel north and cross into the United States illegally to find work.

Most Mexicans prefer not to leave their families for extended periods of time, Bassett explains, nor to live in the shadows of America and in constant fear of deportation. Although an initiative on the scale of

205

this small co-op cannot solve the US-Mexican immigration problem, it is a model for rational and humane solutions to illegal immigration and offers an alternative to spreading the kind of fear and animosity that builds steel fences.

The co-op members are paid about $1.60 per pound for their coffee beans, which is better than Fair Trade standards and roughly three times the 35 to 50 cents per pound that growers are typically paid by commercial buyers. The co-op coffee is shipped north to Agua Prieta, where it is roasted, packaged, and brought across the border to Douglas, where it is sold and distributed throughout the United States to more than five hundred customers in fifty states.

Because the co-op bypasses middlemen and their markups, the fifty coffee-growing families that are involved earn much more than they would otherwise, and the final product, which is organic, can be sold for less than normal prices in the United States. For example, the co-op sells a full pound—a sixteen-ounce bag—of beans or ground coffee for nine or ten dollars, depending on the kind of coffee, rather than the twelve-ounce bags typically sold in supermarkets and coffee shops for that price.

There is a religious component to this project. Although the cooperative is fully Mexican owned and operated, it was launched with seed money from Frontera de Cristo, a border ministry of the Presbyterian Church USA. The cooperative is not a religious group by nature, but devotion is an integral part of the culture and character of life in Salvador Urbina, which has Presbyterian, Catholic, and Jehovah's Witness churches.

## Birth of a Cooperative

As Bassett and I have breakfast at a burrito stand in Agua Prieta, he explains that he first came to the area as a manager at a maquiladora, one of the many foreign-owned assembly plants on the Mexican side of the border that followed the North American Free Trade Agreement of 1994. His company made flexible preprinted circuitry, Bassett says, and grew from 250 employees to 4,000 in just a few years. When the company abandoned Mexico for even cheaper labor in China, Bassett chose to stay and made a career change. He left the business and manufacturing world and joined Frontera de Cristo, which led him to Just Coffee, where he became director of its Just Trade Development Center.

The coffee-growing co-op grew out of the troubling story of Eduardo Perez Verdugo, a coffee grower from Salvador Urbina. In June 1999 Verdugo left his wife and children and traveled north to Agua Prieta to find work in one of the area's maquiladoras. The price of coffee had been steadily dropping, falling from about $130 to only $30 per sack.

"The price of coffee [was] going down and many people [were] leaving and coming north," Verdugo says in a book about the co-op, *Just Coffee: Caffeine with a Conscience*, written by Bassett and Mark Adams. Traveling north was not what Verdugo wanted to do, he explains, because "To leave our land is to suffer." He left in part because his Presbyterian church in Salvador Urbina had been severely damaged by a flood, prompting him and his neighbors to promise they would rebuild it. But it was an impossible task. "I could not both feed my family and raise the money for the church building by picking and selling my coffee."

Verdugo found work in an Agua Prieta factory that produced parts for Ford, Motorola, Toyota, and other companies, earning about forty-seven dollars a week for a forty-eight-hour workweek. That figure approximates the per-*hour* wage of some US auto workers. Although Verdugo only made about one dollar per hour, it was more than he made from his coffee. Then a friend convinced him to cross the US border and take a job working at a golf course in Phoenix, where he could earn ten dollars per hour—more in one day than he could earn per week at the maquiladora. In late October 1999 he made the crossing.

It did not go well. Verdugo twisted an ankle and hurt a knee after falling down an embankment during the night crossing. His group was chased by the US Border Patrol, and because of his injured ankle, he was captured. According to his story, Verdugo was kicked in the face and neck by a border agent. Three days later he was back in Agua Prieta and at the town's Lily of the Valley Presbyterian Church, where he explained his predicament to Adams, the church's minister. If coffee growers could control the price of their coffee, Verdugo said, then people like him would not have to leave their families, their land, and their town. The idea intrigued both Adams and Bassett. Within two years, the cooperative was born.

Daniel Cifuentes, the coffee co-op's director of production, is from one of Salvador Urbina's top coffee-growing families and has been with the co-op since the beginning. Cifuentes guides me and others through the roasting and packing house in Agua Prieta, explaining that the co-op has not veered from the original vision to generate money so "people don't have to migrate to the US to work." Each sack of beans that Cifuentes receives from Salvador Urbina is labeled with the grower's name, the type of coffee, and the style of roast. "What's important is the relationship between the people who produced the coffee and the people who drink it," Cifuentes says. "The people who drink the coffee can know the people who grew it."

The co-op has had a strong impact on life in Salvador Urbina, Cifuentes says. The town now has a water purification system, which treats water at the co-op's office, where it is sold to the community at a very modest price. It has also connected the community with the outside world. "Cell phone service [came to the town] because now people can afford cell phones. Now almost everybody has phone service." The higher prices the co-op pays have helped stabilize the community. "Before, a lot of people left the community. It's now much easier to live there. People who were working undocumented in the US have returned to Salvador Urbina. It's been an economic stimulus for the community."

The higher price paid to co-op producers has also helped non-members bargain better prices from the region's commercial buyers. "Café Justo introduced a new [pricing] model," Cifuentes explains.

"The better price was a just price. Because the coffee is sold [directly] in the north, it is more profitable."

## Into Coffee Country

Later that day, our small group climbs aboard one of Mexico's air-conditioned buses that features continuous movies on small, drop-down screens. The bus rolls out of Agua Prieta and south though the high, dry grasslands of Sonora cattle country and into the sloping, forested mountains. I recall a similar trip I made by bus more than forty years earlier as a university student.

After spending the night in the Sonoran capital of Hermosillo, we take a 6 AM flight to Mexico City, making a connection to the southern Mexican town of Tapachula. It is in the Mexico City airport where I learn of Bassett's deep dedication to the co-op and his disdain for major commercial coffee purveyors such as Starbucks, which he refuses to patronize. Despite Bassett's remarks about Starbucks's coffee, likening it to garbage and accusing the chain of having moved American coffee tastes away from more refined lighter roasts to darker roasts, I sneak a cup anyway.

By mid-afternoon, we arrive in the sparkling airport at Tapachula, a thriving town in the southernmost corner of Chiapas. The air is warm and humid as we load ourselves and our luggage into the back of a couple of pickups driven by co-op members. After a short walk around the center of Tapachula, we take a winding two-lane road into the mountains and soon arrive in Salvador Urbina, a small community spread along a hillside in the shadow of the Tacaná volcano.

At the cooperative's headquarters, we're greeted by the co-op's leader, Reynaldo Cifuentes, the family patriarch. Soon our bags are unloaded and we head off to our various hosts, all coffee-growing families. Bassett and I share a room with extended Cifuentes family members, who live in a comfortable, partly open home on the hillside fronting the co-op headquarters and protected from the frequent rains by a long and sloping roof of corrugated tin. The matriarch of the house is Mama Yoli, an octogenarian who shuffles around the kitchen and ensures that Bassett and I always have fresh coffee.

Bassett and I sit down later with co-op member Elifas Cifuentes to talk about this year's coffee harvest, which is in high gear. Coffee theft can be a big problem, Cifuentes says, especially in years when the harvest is small, so most of the growers have secure rooms in their homes where the burlap and woven plastic sacks of dried and cured coffee beans are kept for sale throughout the year.

Cifuentes explains with a nostalgic smile that Bassett and Adams had a lot of convincing to do before the growers agreed to form the cooperative. Although few liked the low prices paid by commercial buyers, they likewise were unsure that the cooperative could maintain the higher prices being promised. Cifuentes recalls Bassett telling the growers, "If you want to have a business, you have to take risks."

To launch the co-op, Bassett explains, he paid each of the growers three times what they were receiving from the commercial and freelance buyers, known locally as coyotes, the same moniker for the human smugglers along the border. At the time, Bassett says, the coyotes were only paying about thirty dollars for a large sack of beans, and he was paying about a hundred dollars per sack. But for that hundred dollars, Bassett asked each of the growers to give him three bags of beans, two of which would be on consignment. Bassett promised to return in a few months, once the coffee was roasted and sold, and pay them one hundred dollars for each of the two consigned bags. It worked. When Bassett did as he promised, the co-op became a reality.

## Coffee, Coyotes, and Missing Children

As we sit in the shade at David and Lilia Cifuentes's home sipping coffee, both part of the extended coffee-growing Cifuentes family, Lilia tells me why she likes the ten-year-old cooperative. "Before we did not have enough money to pay for workers. Now we do. There's enough money to pay for expenses, but we also have enough money for retirement." With a smile that lights up her careworn face, she says, "When I retire, we will not work. I will stay in my hammock."

Before the co-op began paying higher prices, most coffee growers struggled through the summers until the late fall harvest. Most growers took loans from the commercial buyers that were secured by their pending harvests, but such loans came with exorbitant interest rates. "Now we don't have to do that," Lilia says.

Despite the money that the cooperative generates for the community, it has not stopped young people from going north and crossing into the United States to find work. Some from the Cifuentes family have gone north to pay for the renovations to their homes and to repair damage caused by the region's frequent earthquakes. "When our children go, we don't eat or sleep," David says. "We know it is a dangerous place," because of the Border Patrol, but also the vigilantes. "This is suffering. We don't want our families to leave."

When their son went north looking for work after the roof was blown off part of their house, the family worried when he "didn't call for fifteen days," David says. Their son had paid a coyote $1,500 to cross and was among a group of ten migrants hiding on a hillside during a cold night when the Border Patrol passed by with dogs. But the dogs never picked up on their scent. "The coyote said one of the group was blessed," David explains, "because the Border Patrol missed them. It was the will of God."

Lilia remembers that night as well. "At 4 AM I felt something in my heart," she says. "I woke up and knew he was suffering. I knew that the [Border Patrol] was there. They had dogs. The dogs can smell them." She immediately got out bed, got on her knees, and began to pray that God would protect her son from harm.

Their son made it to Phoenix, David says, and is now part of a landscaping crew. David shows me a photo of the young man operating a small backhoe and says he awaits his son's return so he can take over the family coffee-growing business. His son plans to return once he's made enough money to renovate the home.

The cooperative has helped many of the area's coffee growers from being victimized by the coffee coyotes, Cifuentes explains. Because coffee produces only one crop a year, many of the growers were constantly in debt to the buyers.

"It's hell on cash flow," Bassett says of the coffee growers, who typically must hire pickers to help them harvest. "It's easy to abuse the growers, because you work all year round but only get paid once a year." Because of this, Bassett convinced the cooperative members to sell their coffee on terms and receive payments throughout the year, rather than just once.

The cooperative's price structure is based on fairness, Bassett says. Out of a typical ten-dollar bag of coffee sold in a grocery store or coffee shop, only about fifty cents goes to the grower. Another 30 percent of the sale price goes to the buyers, wholesalers, and others, which leaves about 65 percent profit per bag for the retailer. Considering that a simple cup of black coffee costs about $1.50, and a pound can produce dozens of cups of coffee, "that's a good markup," he says, and means good profits per cup at coffee shops. With most cups of coffee customized with flavors and toppings, the prices and profits are bumped up accordingly.

The cooperative has helped the growers break the cycle of feast and famine, Bassett explains, because "the growers bring [dried coffee] in throughout the year to fulfill their commitment." The cooperative has also freed growers who have been trapped by the coffee-buying coyotes who purchase coffee futures, a specific amount of coffee at a set price, known as a *precio muerto*, or "dead price." If the coffee crop is small and growers can't provide the amount promised, or if the selling price during a harvest season rises above the price the growers agreed to earlier, the growers who sold their crops in advance will suffer. Everyone in the community is affected by the coffee business, Bassett says. "It's a coffee-based economy. It is the source of most of the money that comes into the community."

The cooperative also has allowed the growers to take more time with their coffee plants and plantations to ensure a high quality. "The important thing is the integrity of the growers," Bassett says, if customers want to drink the finest coffees. "A lot of the taste, whether it is bitter or not, depends on the processing."

Most large-scale commercial coffee sellers blend coffees from around the world, Bassett explains, some of which may have been picked years earlier and stored in warehouses. "The traceability is very difficult. You may not know what country or what continent the coffee is from. You could be drinking coffee that is fifteen years old and has been stored in warehouses. The thing with Café Justo is you're drinking last year's coffee."

Although I've learned more about coffee than I ever expected, I realize that I have only begun to scratch the surface as to how closely connected are the people of Mexico and the United States, and yet how separated we have become.

## On the Edge of a Volcano

As Bassett guides our small group of village visitors up the highway into the lush mountains, the towering Tacaná volcano, which rises to 13,333 feet, looms ever closer. We are on our way to the town of El Aguila, or the Eagle, the home of one of the cooperative's most ardent growers, Adán Roblero Mendez. He and his family live on a misty mountainside, where swirling clouds bring a mix of rain and fog, then can suddenly part, revealing a spectacular view of the rolling green foothills that extend almost to the ocean.

Mendez tends his plantation of both fruit and coffee trees, and believes he has one of the best parcels anywhere. "It's not too hot and it's not too cold here," he says with a smile. "The coffee is a little more hardy and has more flavor. The weather here is more rainy" than some other areas nearby. As he hands me a cup of his fresh-brewed coffee, he explains proudly, "The coffee you drink is 100 percent organic."

Mendez's plantation was made possible with money he earned while working and living at a Kentucky thoroughbred horse farm from 1999 to 2003. "They treated me really good," he says. The horse breeder appreciated his workers, telling them that "you have to eat well because I am eating well." Mendez lived as frugally as possible, wiring money to his wife, who supervised the coffee plantation and the building of their home. He had no papers during any of that time, he says.

Getting to Kentucky took some doing. Mendez was stopped in Denver after making his first crossing, and he spent eight days in jail before being taken to Brownsville, Texas, where he was deported to Matamoros, Mexico. Undeterred, he went to Mexico City, then north to Nogales, where he found another coyote to take him into the United States. After crossing far to the west of Nogales with a group of nineteen people, the migrants were attacked by the predatory *bajadores*, who robbed them. "They smelled like marijuana," he says. "We could have killed them, but one of us would have been hurt. So we let them rob us."

Mendez's group walked for many hours after that, stopping whenever they heard strange noises or suspected they had been seen or were being tracked. They eventually reached Interstate 10 and, after a rendezvous with their transporters, rode for three days in a van before reaching the Kentucky horse farm.

"Do you want to go back?" I ask.

He shakes his head and says, "No. We're fine now."

Mendez is proud of his Arabica coffee, though he also grows a lot of Robusta because it requires much less work. Many growers don't bother removing the pulp from the coffee cherries, he says, and sell it *en bola* to the coyote coffee buyers who ply the roads at this time of year. Coffee beans are the seeds found inside the coffee "cherries," he explains, and the sweet pulp that surrounds them must be removed before the beans are dried and roasted. "A lot of people want the money right away. They spend it. What I like about Just Coffee is that the money comes a little bit at a time. That way, we save it and don't spend it all."

Mendez has two sons and a daughter who will eventually return to help run the family coffee business. His oldest son is in the Mexican marines and will most likely retire in another six years. But, he cautions, "the one who will take my place is my wife, Edilma, who loves the business. If I die, she is the one who will take my place."

## Born on a Finca

One of the older members of the cooperative is Alberto "Beto" Sanchez, seventy-eight, who was born and raised and worked on one of the area's German-owned coffee fincas. Sanchez is Catholic and a longtime member of the PRI political party. When he began working on the coffee plantations, it took a half-day to walk to Tapachula. When the road from Tapachula to Salvador Urbina was built in 1964, the coffee-buying coyotes arrived.

Sanchez says he was happy when the Café Justo cooperative was formed. "It worked well from the beginning," Sanchez says. "The coyotes were offering really low prices for the coffee. We made a commitment [to the co-op] back then because the price offered was three times that of the coyotes. I am really content and happy because of the price of the coffee, and the price keeps increasing." Sanchez says his son, Diego, has taken over his coffee business, but this has created some family tensions, he says, because his daughters also want to continue to be part of and profit from the business.

The cooperative is helping members by providing young starter coffee trees and offering varieties to strengthen the mixture of harvest. "Before the cooperative, our eyes were closed," Diego says, and many in the town dreamed only of leaving the community and going to the United States to work. Now he and at least six or seven others his age have remained in the community and have taken over their families' coffee businesses.

Sanchez's seventy-one-year-old wife, Benita, who is an integral part of the family's coffee business, remembers the day she first saw her future husband. "He was working and carrying coffee," she says. "I saw him and liked him." They have ten children, Diego being the oldest. "There are many who want to be part of the cooperative," Benita says, "but they want to receive the payments right away," and so they sell to the coffee coyotes. When locals see cooperative members receiving money year-round for their coffee, "some are envious," she adds. "If Café Justo goes away, we will go back to the way we were," she says wistfully. "We were suffering from low prices."

At the urging of her family, Benita shows off a small crown and silk sash she was awarded for being a princess in this year's coffee festival, or feria, celebrated in Salvador Urbina during each harvest. Rather than selecting the festival queen through a beauty pageant, this year the organizers made the event a benefit for the community kindergarten.

Grandmothers were asked to raise money for the school, and the one who raised the most money was crowned queen of the feria. "People wanted me to be the queen," Benita says, "but I wasn't because the other women raised more money." Benita collected 5,000 pesos, or about $385, while the queen raised 7,000 pesos, or about $540. Life has changed in Salvador Urbina from when she was young. "I used to be more joyful," Benita says. "Everything used to be cheaper." But she still enjoys the annual feria. "I really enjoy dancing," she says.

An additional multigenerational impact of the Café Justo co-op is explained later that day when I meet with another of the cooperative's founding members, Guadalupe Morales Trejo, fifty-nine. For the past six years, because of the increased income provided by the co-op, Trejo has been able to employ a full-time person to help maintain his coffee farm and then to hire at least three others, usually Guatemalans, to help bring in the harvest. This year's weather has been good for the Robusta coffee trees, Trejo says, and he is looking forward to good profits.

The cooperative's prices have saved a lot of people from selling their land, Trejo says. "If you wanted to give your children an education, you needed to sell some of your land." But no more, Trejo says. "I'm used to the payment plan. It guarantees that I'll have money year-round." With a better income, he sent two of his daughters to nursing school, and his son has become a chemist. "It was easy for me at the school. It required monthly payments. I didn't need to sell my land. They are working and I have my land."

## The Guatemalan Pickers

For the past week, Bassett and I have been staying in the home of Isaac Cifuentes, son of Café Justo leader Reynaldo Cifuentes. Since it is harvest time, Isaac has been rising early to take the pickers to his coffee parcels, where he supervises the harvest. At breakfast one morning, Isaac confides to me that he plans to go to the United States once the harvest is finished to find work in Atlanta, home to a growing Hispanic community and an enclave from Salvador Urbina.

Also in Isaac's house and sharing a back bedroom are four Guatemalan coffee pickers who have been working with Cifuentes for the past month and who will continue with him until the harvest is complete. Room and board for the pickers is part of their pay. When I accompany Isaac to his coffee land parcels, I watch as the Guatemalans work quickly, using both hands to strip the ripe red and green coffee bean cherries from the branches and put them into large woven baskets tied to their waists. Typically working from sunrise to about 2 PM each day, they fill two large sacks per day and are paid by the amount they pick.

Much of the coffee in this area is picked by such Guatemalan laborers who cross the border into Mexico without working papers, duplicating the situation of Mexican workers crossing into the United States to work for much higher wages than can be earned in their own country.

"We get paid better," says David Velasquez, twenty-six, who with his friends has come to Mexico for the past several years to pick coffee. "It's a big help." They come from a small community of about a thousand families in the mountains not far from San Marcos, Guatemala, which is about sixty miles east of Salvador Urbina. Coffee, along with corn, bananas, and papaya, are grown around their hometown, but few people have jobs, they complain. "We don't have a choice,"

Velasquez says. "There is no work, so we need to come here." Each will take home about $150 for two months' work.

Gang and drug violence is bad in Guatemala, they say, but is concentrated in the bigger cities, not the countryside, where drugs and drug trafficking are not a problem. None have work permits, only travel documents.

Omar Cardon, twenty, the youngest of the group, has picked coffee in Salvador Urbina for the past seven years—since he was thirteen years old.

"Do you want to go to the US to work?" I ask.

"A lot of people are working in the US," Cardon says of his acquaintances, "but not us. It's hard [to make the trip] and it costs money." To go to the United States one must come from a family with some money, they explain. Few in rural areas can afford to pay the thousands of dollars that crossing into the United States requires.

"Of course we want to go," says Anibal Lopez, twenty-eight, another of the pickers, "but we don't have money. And we know the situation with the Border Patrol." He and his friends are desperate for work, Lopez says, since they don't have enough land to farm or even grow a large garden, which requires money to buy seeds and cultivation tools.

They spend what little money they have on food and water, Lopez says. They typically live in wooden homes with packed dirt floors and use outhouses for sanitation. None of them were born in a hospital, and there is no doctor in their town. The recent earthquakes in Guatemala, the aftereffects of which are felt during our visit, caused some damage to their town, but most people survived. "Some houses fell over," Lopez says, but no one died.

## So Close and Yet So Far

When Bassett, I, and the others arrive at the Tapachula airport before dawn for our return trip, we learn that our flight to Mexico City, where we are to make a connection north to Hermosillo, has been canceled. Another plane arrives six hours later, which takes us to Mexico City by mid-afternoon—too late to make our connection. The airline offers accommodations for the night and a shuttle to and from the airport. After a meal at the hotel's buffet, we head for the Zócalo, the historic plaza in the heart of the city.

We take the city's underground metro, a complex system of interconnecting lines that serves the sprawling megalopolis of more than twenty million people. It is late Saturday afternoon and the metro is crowded, colorful, and raw. Young men with blaring CD players strapped to their backs meander among the cars, peddling their CDs, as others sell the ubiquitous packets of gum.

We emerge from underground into the cool, dark evening of the Zócalo, milling with people preparing for the annual Revolution Day celebration on the next Monday. Dim memories of my college days in Mexico City from forty-five years ago fill my mind. One that haunts me is of an impoverished elderly woman crawling across the stone and concrete on her knees toward the majestic Metropolitan Cathedral, crying and stopping every few feet to bow her head in prayer. I had never before seen such devotion. This evening, no such devotees are evident. I step inside the chapel beside the cathedral where people crowd the Saturday evening Mass, a brightly lit event with sonorous prayers and chants.

On the exterior of one of the large buildings facing the Zócalo are depictions of two of Mexico's revolutionary heroes, Emiliano Zapata and Pancho Villa, their hats, faces, and stylized mustaches outlined in bright lights at one hundred times life-size. Vilified by America and having died at the hands of an assassin, Villa remains a national symbol of defiance of authority and a champion of the peasantry, along with his contemporary Zapata.

Rather than returning by the crowded metro, I and a couple of others climb into a taxi and head back to the hotel, hoping that Mexico's congested traffic has eased. We immediately strike up a conversation with the young driver, Luis, who, when he learns we are Americans, explains that he just returned from four years working and living as an undocumented prep cook in the kitchen of an Italian restaurant in

Chicago. He never learned English, he says, yet lived in Chicago with his wife and two young children, who attended school and learned English.

He returned to Mexico after his wife insisted that her children grow up with family. Crossing the border into the United States is not a big deal, Luis says, because so many people do it, all for the same reason: to make money. He made it to the States after buying clothes and supplies in Altar, Sonora, just as those who were captured had done when I traveled with the Border Patrol. Luis has relatives in Denver, Colorado, he says, and he would not hesitate to return to the United States if he needs money again.

The next day, we catch an early flight from Mexico City to Hermosillo, and as we wait, Bassett points out a group of men waiting to board the flight who are probably planning to cross into the United States. They all have the telltale look, Bassett says, and are wearing jeans, warm jackets, and sturdy shoes and carrying backpacks but no luggage. Bassett has made this trip and this flight many times and says this flight often has been packed with people preparing to cross into the United States.

When we land in Hermosillo, the men are indeed met by their coyotes and immediately directed to cars and vans that whisk them away, quite possibly to Altar, which is about 125 miles northwest, where they will stage their US entry.

Later that night we also cross into the United States. After saying good-bye and buying about five pounds of Café Justo coffee, I climb into my car and head back to Tucson. Hungry and needing gas for my car, I pull into a Circle K store in the town of Sierra Vista, which is just fifteen miles north of the Mexican border, and buy a sandwich, a bag of chips, and bottled water. When I pull change out of my pocket, I have several Mexican coins in my hand. The eighteen-year-old clerk sees them and excitedly asks, "What kind of money is that!" I hand him a peso, explaining that it's Mexican. He looks on in amazement, turns it in his fingers, then thanks me when I give it to him.

I am dumbstruck at his question and its implications. This young man has been living just fifteen miles from the border yet has never seen Mexican money? No wonder such a gulf of misunderstanding exists in the borderlands. Despite the proximity of the people on both sides of the US-Mexico border, there is a deplorable lack of interaction, unfortunately fueled by fear and ignorance. I climb back into my car and drive into the night.

A couple of days later as I am leaving Tucson to return to Colorado, I get a taste of the deeply rooted anti-Mexican fervor that permeates Arizona. I tune in to AM talk radio and come across a couple of announcers discussing Arizona's ban on Mexican American studies in public schools.

"It's going to destroy Tucson," one of the hosts says of Mexican American studies. Proponents of such studies are biased, one says, not the opponents, because ethnic studies focus on just one group, not the broader society. "You're not racist" for supporting the Mexican studies ban, he says. "They're racist." He then adds, "They're trying to shame you into thinking you're racist." Incensed by reports that some schoolteachers were defying the ban, the other host urges listeners to get active, attend rallies, and pressure public schools to enforce the ban. American "values are under assault," a host says. "It's really anti-American studies."

Although ethnic studies grew out of federal desegregation rulings decades ago, which called for equal education to all students, the Arizona legislature in 2010 passed HB 2811, which banned Mexican American studies, claiming that the courses promoted racism against non-Hispanic whites and supported ethnic solidarity that some said might lead to the overthrow of the government. In 2013, however, again based on desegregation rulings, a federal court would order the Tucson school district to resume its Mexican American studies at the high school level, along with African American studies.

## Epilogue

# BORDERLINE REALITIES

❋

**Preconceived notions, illusions if you will,** often influence actions more than hard, cold reality. Such is the case with the US-Mexico border. This was clear when I paused on a hillside in the desert scrublands south of Tucson, Arizona, and witnessed the plight of a lost, frightened, and thoroughly disoriented young man from Guatemala. Separated from the coyote who had brought him and his friends into the United States, this man wanted nothing more than to go home. He sensed that if he continued to wander the desert highlands as he had been doing for three days, he could die. Dashed were his dreams of a better life in New York City, where he expected to work as a manual laborer.

This man was a threat to no one. Yet the United States has established a quasimilitary force of some twenty thousand men and women patrolling the border with Mexico that requires the expenditure of tens of billions of dollars each year to protect this country against people like him. This threat verges on being irrational if not illusory. At its core is a primordial wariness of "the other," an evolutionary defense mechanism still at work in the human brain.

In the case of the US-Mexico border, the increasingly frantic calls for ever higher amounts of security to protect America against an invasion of "illegals"—in large measure brown-skinned people—is little more than what the Southern Poverty Law Center calls "Mexican bashing." Considering that few similar security measures have been taken along the US-Canadian border, which is twice as long as the US-Mexico border and some say presents a more serious risk, the annual expenditure of billions along America's southern border illustrates an anti-Mexican bias fed by fearmongering.

From the beginning of my investigations, I sought to explain why and how the US-Mexico border situation had evolved to what it is now. Since the United States and Mexico have shared a border, a history, and a culture for centuries, I suspected that solutions might be self-evident. They are. But only if one can get beyond the bigotry and misinformation that far too often dominates immigration and border debate.

The explanation for the current border situation is that everything changed after al-Qaeda's attacks on the United States of September 11, 2001. Indeed it did. That fateful day I was in Yerevan, Armenia, and had just returned from my daily run along the Hrazdan River valley road that cuts through the city. I turned on CNN to see flames and black smoke streaming from the Twin Towers, mesmerized as CNN replayed the passenger jets crashing into them. The entire world was shocked at the spectacle. America, the country that embodies the hopes and ambitions of the world, was burning. In the days that followed, many humble Armenians laid bouquets of flowers on the sidewalk in front of the US embassy.

The American response was predictable. Going after Osama bin Laden, the mastermind of the attacks, was of course necessary. But when bin Laden slipped away and disappeared into Pakistan, where he lived in hiding until his death in May 2011 at the hands of American commandoes, the United States embarked on a seven-year war in Iraq, even though Iraq had neither weapons of mass destruction nor anything to do with the attacks of 9/11.

As money, machinery, and military might were directed against Iraq, the recently created Homeland Security Department absorbed the country's border protection agencies. Attention quickly turned to the US-Mexican border. A border fence was ordered in 2006 to stem out-of-control migrations from Mexico into the United States, and several thousand national guardsmen were sent to help fight the "alien invasion."

This was done despite the fact that, just as with Iraq and the Iraqis, neither Mexico nor the Mexican people had anything to do with the attacks of 9/11. Yet Mexico's migrants have been vilified by vigilante groups, border security advocates, and high-ranking public officials as a terrorist-like threat to the integrity and security of the United States. As an estimated seven hundred miles of fencing was being thrown up along the two-thousand-mile border, the flames of ethnic hatred were being fanned even as an estimated twelve million undocumented workers, mostly from Mexico, were already living in this country and contributing to the US economy.

The blurred distinctions between Mexico's migrant workers and jihadi terrorists were apparent as I wandered the aisles of the exhibition hall at the border security conference in El Paso in the fall of 2012. Hardening of the US-Mexico border lurched forward despite the fact that no terrorists have been captured at that border and even as one of the nation's top security analysts explained that the unguarded and unpatrolled four-thousand-mile Canadian border posed a more likely terrorist entry point.

There is precedent to this attitude and activity. America went to war with Mexico in 1846, a conflict that ended in 1848 with Mexico's northern territories becoming the American Southwest, fulfilling America's "manifest destiny." A largely forgotten chapter in US history, the war with Mexico was followed by a similar military invasion seventy years later, an abortive expedition to capture the revolutionary leader Pancho Villa for his destructive 1916 raid on Columbus, New Mexico.

America's modern notions of Mexico are driven largely by a refusal to face the reality of its historical and true relationship with that country: that the United States and its people and policies have contributed significantly to what most see as only Mexico's problems.

Mexican cartels rose as US antinarcotics efforts precipitated the demise of the South American cocaine cartels. But this did nothing to slake America's thirst for illegal drugs, estimated at more than $100 billion a year. America's demand for drugs was and is being met by the nearest, most readily available suppliers—Mexican cartels.

America must acknowledge its role in the development of the Mexican drug cartels and their perpetuation through a system of drug laws based on misconceptions, not the least of which has to do with mild narcotics such as marijuana, as exemplified by the 1936 cult classic movie *Reefer Madness*. US drug laws have created a virulent and highly profitable drug underground that thrives on both sides of the border. Decriminalizing the possession of marijuana, if not outright legalization, as has been adopted by some states, is a step in the right direction.

America also must take an introspective look at its demand for narcotics. Improved mental health care and services can help reduce the country's drug addictions. Cutting the demand, as was done with tobacco use, is the surest, healthiest, and least expensive approach. It is also the most effective way to undermine the power of the drug cartels while helping the government of Mexico regain control of its runaway crime problem.

One of America's most disturbing disconnects from the Mexican reality is the staggering death toll that has been exacted on the Mexican people by the bloody fighting among Mexican drug cartels. The uproar around the Fast and Furious gun-tracking debacle exposed that tens of thousands, if not hundreds of thousands, of high-powered weapons made and sold by Americans have ended up in the hands of cartel killers. US gun makers and dealers have pocketed millions of dollars by providing these weapons, which are banned in Mexico, enabling cartels to carry out their reign of terror against the Mexican people and their government. From seventy to ninety thousand people in Mexico have lost their lives at the hands of cartel killers. Yet America's secondary role in these deaths is wholly ignored.

Yet another disconnect from reality is the assertion that the influx of low-skilled, low-paid labor from Mexico is dragging down the American economy. The opposite is true. That much of America's farm produce is picked by low-wage earners means that America's fruit, vegetables, dairy, and even its meat products can be sold in grocery stores at lower prices than would otherwise be possible. Thousands of restaurants across the country employ undocumented workers who prepare the food Americans eat and clean the dishes on which it is served. These workers help hold down prices. The same is true of the millions of undocumented workers who fill the crews that build houses, nail on roofs, landscape lawns, tend greenhouses, and manicure golf courses.

The Internal Revenue Service has estimated that some six million undocumented workers file individual income tax returns each year. The Congressional Budget Office has noted that undocumented workers, like all consumers in America, pay state and local sales taxes. Studies show that undocumented workers have paid at least $7 billion per year into the Social Security fund, as reported in a 2005 article by Eduardo Porter in the *New York Times*, a benefit they will never collect. These contributions by undocumented workers to Social Security and Medicare bolster the benefits for older Americans.

In 2006 Carole Keeton Strayhorn, the Texas comptroller, wrote in a report on the economic impact of immigrants that "the absence of the estimated 1.4 million undocumented immigrants in Texas in fiscal 2005 would have been a loss to our gross state product of $17.7 billion. Undocumented immigrants produced $1.58 billion in state revenues, which exceeded the $1.16 billion in state services they received. However, local governments bore the burden of $1.44 billion in uncompensated health care costs and local law enforcement costs not paid for by the state."

Although the US-Mexico border needs to be secure, a sealed border does not solve the immigration or drug problem, nor does it remove the strong economic incentives that many Mexicans and Central Americans have for crossing the border illegally. Building a fence, in fact, may be counterproductive. In an era of austere national budgets, estimates are that a fence along the entire two-thousand-mile border would cost about $23 billion. Instead of spending that much money on what would be America's version of the Berlin Wall, money would be better spent on economic development projects in Mexico so fewer people are compelled to cross the border to find work.

If there is one major solution to the Mexican migration problem it would be to create a sweeping guest worker visa program that could be funded with a portion of the estimated $23 billion it would cost to seal off the border. Such a visa program would allow the twelve million people who now live and work in the United States illegally to be recognized for fulfilling a need and contributing to the economy. Such a program would also allow migrant workers to return to their home countries without the fear that they might never again be able to work in the United States. It makes no sense to keep these people in the shadows and pretend they don't exist or are not part and parcel of the American economy.

There are other reasons for such a visa program. One is that it would help release the stranglehold that drug cartels now have on illegal immigration. The cartels charge about $3,000 per person to cross. If each of the estimated one million migrants who cross the border each year paid that amount, it means that human smuggling from Mexico into the United States is a $3-billion-per-year business. With this amount of cash in hand, the human smugglers have massive resources to ensure success, regardless of the US Border Patrol. If the Mexicans and Central Americans seeking work in the United States could do so legally, it would take $3 billion annually out of the hands of the cartels.

Current immigration policy has had the opposite effect of its intent, making it difficult for the undocumented to leave the United States. They know it will be dangerous and costly to return to the United States because of the control drug cartels have on human smuggling and the increasingly likelihood of capture and incarceration. As a result, most chose to remain in the United States, living in the shadows, ever fearful of arrest, deportation, and separation from their families. Current immigration policy has created a permanent underclass in America.

The recent spate of anti-immigrant laws in the United States has been reactionary, xenophobic, and counterproductive. As the farmers in Alabama and Georgia complained in the wake of their state's ill-advised anti-immigration laws, they need Mexico's migrant workforce to harvest their crops. Residents in those states, who apparently are unwilling to do the work, make the case for an extensive guest worker visa program all the more compelling. Yet present law primarily punishes the undocumented while barely slapping the wrists of the thousands of employers who hire them. If stanching the flow of illegal immigration is truly the goal, then fairness demands that sanctions and penalties be placed on those who knowingly hire the undocumented.

One of the most important yet least-discussed issues in the border and immigration debate is the effectiveness of border security measures. Has the massive expansion of the US Border Patrol's budget and personnel stemmed the tide of illicit border crossings? Based on the data available, the answer is no. The Border Patrol routinely issues statistics on the number of migrants apprehended annually. When numbers steadily dropped from a high of about 1.6 million a decade ago to just about 357,000 in the year ending September 2012, success was declared. Many along the border remained unconvinced, however, and argued that economic issues are the governing factor, not border security, although security certainly must play a role. Recent data appears to support the enforcement critics. Total apprehensions for the year ending September 2013 were 420,000, a major rise in illegal migration that could be attributed to economic reasons, despite bigger border security budgets.

In addition, the decline in border apprehensions over the past decade begs the question: while many migrants are apprehended, how many are not? One answer can be found in studies by Princeton University's Mexican Migrant Project (http://mmp.opr.princeton.edu /home-en.aspx). Based on interviews with thousands of people from migrant communities, the apprehension rate has hovered around 30 percent of those crossing the border. In 2007 the rate rose to about 50 percent, but by 2011 it had reversed direction and dropped to less than 25 percent. That means a migrant stands a 75 percent chance of successfully crossing into the United States illegally. The Princeton University data suggests that if the Border Patrol caught 327,000 people in 2011, and it was only about a quarter of all who crossed, then nearly one million migrants actually entered the United States. If the success rate is applied to the 357,000 apprehended in 2012, then another one million crossed into the United States that year as well.

This crossing rate undermines the argument for more and better border security as a way to address illegal immigration. It casts serious doubts on the effectiveness of bigger fences, of thousands more Border Patrol agents, and billions of dollars more for border security budgets. What is the point of diminishing returns? The hard and cold facts show that increasing expenditures for border security is the wrong approach. Throwing good money after bad makes no sense.

Can a perfectly secure border be achieved? Is that what America wants and needs? If the answer to either question is no, it negates the insistence by border security advocates that the US-Mexico border must first be sealed before immigration can be reformed. If the goal of a totally secure border is unattainable and may not be desirable, then the only sensible solution *is* immigration reform.

America's approach to the border, however, is going in the opposition direction. An example is America's unnecessarily heavy-handed approach to immigration enforcement, which was revealed in late March 2013 when the US Immigration and Customs Enforcement agency admitted to using solitary confinement in about three hundred immigrant cases during a five-month period in 2012. The agency oversees the sprawling and largely privately operated prisons for apprehended migrants. America's use of solitary confinement, albeit in relatively few cases, has drawn criticism from people such as Juan Méndez, United National special rapporteur on torture, as being tantamount to cruel and unusual punishment.

We are a nation of immigrants. We should pause for a moment to consider the Statue of Liberty that holds the torch of freedom high over the harbor in New York City. As America moves forward with immigration reform, we must recall our roots. America is not the land of closed doors and prisons cells—it is the land of opportunity. This truth must not be forgotten as the United States reconsiders its immigration policies and determines the fate of the twelve million undocumented people among us who are realizing their American dream, the same dream we all hold dear.

# INDEX

※

**233**